NOONTIDE
AT
SYCHAR

NOONTIDE
AT
SYCHAR

A New Testament Chapter
in Procidence and Grace

(The story of Jacob's well)

By

John MacDuff

Bottom of the Hill Publishing
Memphis, TN
www.BottomoftheHillPublishing.com

ISBN: 978-1-61203-769-1

Content

THE NEEDS BE

"He had to go through Samaria." John 4:4

In the previous chapter (the companion book Eventide at Bethel) we considered some of the outward accessories in this beautiful and instructive narrative of the Apostle of Love, and grouped together a number of historical associations and personal recollections which may serve to vivify the spiritual lessons which will henceforth claim our attention. John's narration forms one of those episodes in the life of his divine Master, full of circumstantial details, which are peculiar to himself. It reminds us of another and similar chapter of his Gospel—his domestic portraiture, touched with so delicate a hand, of the family of Bethany, and which, as in the present case, he alone of the four evangelists has delineated—"apples of gold in pictures of silver."

There is much interesting material to invite attention without further premise, but one preliminary incidental remark on the threshold of the Evangelist's narrative must claim our consideration in the present chapter—*"He had to go through Samaria."*

Samaria lay in the direct route between Judea and Galilee. There was, indeed, an alternative road by the eastern side of the Jordan valley and Perea. But the former, for various reasons, was most frequently traversed then, as it is invariably now; and that, too, notwithstanding the indignities, to which we shall subsequently allude, which the Galileans had often to encounter in the transit, owing to the hostility of the lawless mixed tribe inhabiting the valleys around Ebal and Gerizim. Josephus specially mentions that the pilgrim Hebrews from northern Palestine, in going to their anniversary festivals in Jerusalem, preferred this shorter journey, although these were the very occasions when the spirit of malignant and inveterate enmity between the conflicting races was most violently expressed. If this, then, were the favorite, most usual, most frequented highway between Jerusalem and Nazareth, does it not seem, unless for some specific reason, to be redundant phraseology, (and more especially as addressed to readers who were thoroughly conversant with the itineraries of their own country) for the Evangelist so strongly to assert in his narrative the axiomatic fact as to the "had to" or necessity laid upon Christ to go to Galilee by the ordinary route? Moreover, from a subsequent statement (ver. 40) it could not have been purposes of expedition which in His case made this route imperative, as we find He was induced so far to alter what seemed His original intention, by tarrying at Shechem for "two days."

What then was this divine constraint imposed upon the adorable Redeemer which demanded so special an entry in the narrative of the inspired recorder? We answer, it was because of an occurrence registered in an older and more majestic volume—the *Book of the Divine decrees.* 'By the determinate counsel and foreknowledge of God,' a wandering star was, in the course of this memorable journey, to be reclaimed from its devious orbit, and a glorious testimony given as to *how God's sovereign grace can triumph over all obstacles*, and be independent of all place and circumstance.

To no locality could the Great Sower have 'gone forth to sow,' with the prospect of more *un*promising results, than to that morally and spiritually rocky and thorny wayside. "Thorns had come up everywhere, the ground was covered with weeds, and the stone wall was in ruins," (Prov. 24:31) It had acquired an evil reputation. The very name, *Shechem*, had, by common parlance, been merged into the disgraceful epithet "Sychar," which means "drunkard" or "folly." It was one of Jeroboam's cities—the wicked prince whose name has been cursed with the unenviable notoriety that "he made Israel to sin." Perhaps it may have been the dreadful depravity, and, humanly speaking, invulnerable unbelief of the Samaritan race which dictated the Savior's earliest commission to His yet untried disciples, "Do not go among the Gentiles or enter any town of the Samaritans. Go rather to the lost sheep of Israel," (Matt. 10:5, 6.)

What, however, deters the servant is not to deter the Master. "Who are you, O great mountain?" Before the true Zerubbabel you shall become a plain. The wisdom of God is not "Sychar:" it is wiser than men, and the weakness of God is stronger than men. In the midst of drunkards and debauchees the Christ of Nazareth is to prove and vindicate the omnipotence of that divine energy which can change the vulture into the dove, the lion into the lamb, and bring the outcast of Shechem, like the demoniac of Gadara, to sit submissive at His feet. In the glowing figure of the prophet, these mountains around are to break forth before him into singing, and all the trees of the field are to clap their hands: instead of the thorn, is to come up the fir tree; and instead of the briar, is to come up the myrtle tree. His own declaration by the lips of the same seer is to receive a remarkable fulfillment in the case of the Church of Samaria, and especially in her who was *the first ingathered sheaf*, "I revealed Myself to those who did not ask for me; I was found by those who did not seek Me. To a nation that did not call on My name, I said, 'Here am I, here am I.'"

Need we wonder now, at the apparently superfluous entry in the Gospel narrative, "He HAD to go through Samaria?" What would the infant Church, yes, the Church in all ages, have missed, had our Bibles been stripped of this fourth chapter of John? A sweet, silver tone of the jubilee trumpet would have been lost to the trembling, the despairing, the perishing. Oh most memorable incident! Oh most honored fountain! Well may the 'Israel of God' stand round the stony margin—as did the Hebrew nobles and princes of old with their rugged staves, at Beer, on the borders of Moab, by the brooks of Arnon—and say, in the words of that oldest pilgrim song, "Spring up, O well: sing to it," for a nobler than Hebrew "prince" or "noble" has made you oracular—put a tongue into your depths—and made you speak of "living water springing up into everlasting life."

There is one special practical thought which this "had to" of the great wayside Traveler suggests: it is, **the peerless value of a single soul in the sight of Christ.**

It is the truth of His own exquisite parable exhibited in impressive reality: the heavenly Shepherd, when, out of the hundred sheep He had missed *one* erring wanderer, going amid these mountains of *Samaria* to seek 'that which was lost.' There were many in populous *Jerusalem* to whom we might have expected rather that He would have borne the water of life, crowds of far more willing and receptive hearers were in the district of Aenon, near to Salim, the scene of the Baptist's successful labors. In His own city of Capernaum were waiting responsive multitudes—many who had long sat in gross darkness, but who now saw and owned the great Light—friends of the Bridegroom, who were rejoicing greatly because of the Bridegroom's voice. But on His way there, *the sigh of one lone captive* is borne to His ear—the bleat of one truant of the flock, fleece-torn, and footsore, and weary, is heard under the shadow of Ebal, or rather under the shadow of those curses which of old rang from Ebal's frowning rocks—for the sake of that *one*, not an inspired penman, not a recording angel, but His own infinite love and mercy dictates the words, "He had to go!"

Nor is this a solitary example given us in Scripture of the *priceless estimate put by the Divine Being on the worth of one soul.* Take as another illustrative case, that of the **Ethiopian eunuch** traveling through the desert of Gaza; a case all the more suitable as having a topographical connection with the Church in Samaria, of which this woman was the honored founder. That prime minister or chief treasurer of the Queen of Ethiopia, a Jewish proselyte—like the Hadjis one meets so often still in the East coming from the shrine of the false prophet at Mecca, or like the Greek and Russian pilgrims returning from their pilgrimages to Jerusalem—was proceeding homewards from the Hebrew 'city of solemnities' (Jerusalem), where he had been doing homage to the one living and true God. Despite, however, his renunciation of the polytheism of Ethiopia; despite his formal subscription to the creed of Judaism, and the earnestness and sincerity evinced by his undertaking that vast journey from Africa to Asia, it is evident that he was retracing his steps still a stranger to peace; the deep longing of his soul had been umnet and unsatisfied. It seemed as if in vain he had braved for weeks, hot suns by day, and drenching dews by night. But unlike the hardened, indifferent Samaritan woman of our narrative, he had been in the way of duty. Unlike her, he had been *seeking* the living water, although he had failed to find it, and was returning in his chariot scanning the scroll of the great prophet, which was opened at the most glorious and gladdening of Isaiah's gospel visions. He had gone as a worshiper to Pentecost; and although his eyes continued blinded to those elevating verities of a new dispensation, which alone could give him light and life, he was still cherishing and manifesting the child-like spirit of a devout inquirer. This Ethiopian was "stretching forth his hands to God"—"seeking the Lord, if perhaps he might find Him." "Blessed are those who hunger and thirst after righteousness, for they shall be filled."

At that time a new life had stirred Samaria's valley of dry bones. Living streams had reached it better than those which had made a little material Paradise of the adjoining glens of Ephraim and Manasseh: the thirsty spiritual land had become pools of water. Philip the Evangelist had been specially sent to this scene of revival. He was preaching with acceptance; hundreds were hanging on his lips: for we read, "Philip went down to the city of Samaria and proclaimed Christ there; When the crowds heard Philip and saw the miraculous signs he did, they all paid close attention to what he said. . . So there was great joy in the city." This religious awakening, commencing in Samaria as the capital, extended among the surrounding villages and towns; Shechem doubtless participated in the shower that had come down in its season—the "shower of blessing." In the midst of his career of usefulness, an angel—a delegate from the upper sanctuary—is sent on a special mission to this greatly owned and successful minister of God. Strange to say, it is to arrest him in the field of his abundant labor, just when he is scattering the good seed with bounteous hand, and seeing it springing up under the rain and dews of heaven. It is a mandate, however, from which there can be no evasion, and he immediately obeys the summons. But what is this new sphere of more imperative duty? Why are these souls, hungering for the bread of life, left all at once without assistance? why these fields abandoned for the time by this faithful reaper, just when inviting the sickle, already "white unto the harvest?" It is, that one weary spirit may be comforted; that one stray sheaf may be gathered into the heavenly garner; and not until that solitary traveler in the Gaza desert is sent on his way rejoicing, does Philip return to his labors.

Yes, we again say, reverting to the narrative of John, beautiful testimony to the yearning *personal* love of the Savior. "He had to go;" and that 'necessity' was to polish one stone for the building of His temple, one gem for the embellishment of His crown—to give to one shipwrecked abandoned vessel, drifting fast to destruction amid wild tempests and wintry seas, rest and safety and repose in the haven of His own infinitely pure presence and compassion. It reminds one of what is so often seen, and is always so touching, a mother's tender affection for her pining invalid—the weary suffering inhabitant of the sick-chamber—the caged bird of the family, with drooping wing and wailing note and ruffled plumage. The hardier plants are left to battle with the storm; but her most tender care is lavished on the sickly flower prematurely drooping. The others are for the time forgotten, as she watches the blanching of these tender leaves, the early falling of these cherished blossoms. Or more touching still, when with bated breath she speaks of the blank in her household, and how, with all her gratitude for remaining blessings, her heart of hearts wanders to the silent churchyard after that which was lost!

"My brothers, if one of you (any *one* of you) should wander from the truth and someone should bring him back, remember this: Whoever turns a sinner from the error of his way will save him from death and cover over a multitude of sins." "In the same way, I tell you, there is rejoicing in the presence of the angels of God over ONE sinner who repents."

God still "sets the solitary in families, and brings out those who are bound with chains." Is there not the richest and most tender encouragement here for the guiltiest? The "had to" which brought the Savior of the world to that wayside well of old, may bring Him still, in His ineffable compassion, to the chief of sinners—to manifest the same divine solicitude, the same personal love. Let none deem themselves beyond the pale of His divine power and sympathy and support, as if that great Central Sun had lost its sovereign control over the wandering star plunging amid the ever-deepening darkness; or as if He had altered or modified His own saying, which in this narrative passage has received so sublime an illustration—"I came not to call the righteous, but sinners to repentance." Rather, as with your eye on the well of Sychar, and on the compassion and pity garnered in the divine heart, you exclaim, "Can it be that He will receive 'ME, *even* ME?'" go, turn the words of the simple but beautiful hymn into a prayer—

"Pass me not, O gracious Father,
Sinful though my heart may be;
You might leave me, but the rather
Let Your mercy light on me—
Even *me.*

"Pass me not, O tender Savior—
Let me live and cling to Thee—
I am longing for Your favor;
While You are calling, call for me—
Even *me.*

"Have I long in sin been sleeping—
Long been slighting, grieving Thee?
Has the world my heart been keeping?
Oh, forgive and rescue me!
Even *me.*

"Love of God so pure and changeless,
Blood of Christ so rich and free,
Grace of God so strong and boundless,
Magnify it all in me—
Even *me.*

"Pass me not—this lost one bringing,
Bind my heart, O Lord, to Thee;
While the streams of life are springing,
Gladden others—gladden me!
Even me."

THE WEARY PILGRIM

"Jesus, tired as He was from the journey, sat thus down by the well. It was about the sixth hour." John 4:6

Nothing more frequently impressed the writer while sojourning in Palestine, than a feature in the humiliation of our blessed Lord which never so much as occurred previously—the *bodily fatigue* which He must have constantly undergone in His often pilgrimages along arid plains and sultry valleys. If even now, with all the comforts of tent and equipage, the modern traveler finds walking oppressive and exhausting, what must it have been to traverse these, with no aid but the staff and rough sandal. The Ethiopian eunuch, referred to in the preceding chapter, traveling through the desert of Gaza, was "sitting in his chariot." We picture Abraham, or his grandson who dug the well of Sychar, as they came and went from Mesopotamia or Hebron, mounted on their camels, with "all the substance they had gotten" following in long file; but, He, whose day they saw afar off and were glad, seems on all occasions, except one, to have journeyed on foot; that one (the Hosanna entrance) being an exceptional public assertion of His theocratic and royal rights as Zion's king. While the pilgrim father of old, and the pilgrim wayfarer still, pitch their canvas or goatskin tents, this Lord of pilgrims was content to spread His garment of camel's hair under the shade of some fig tree or thorny nook; or perchance within one of the abounding natural caverns in the limestone rock, He would catch a few hours of broken slumber, either when night drew its curtains around Him, or, as is the used of travelers and caravans still, during the sultry heat of noon. Often in His own touching words, (among the most touching He ever spoke,) 'the foxes had holes, and the birds of the air had nests, but the Son of man had nowhere to lay His head.'

It is such a picture which is now brought before us in the course of our narrative—"Jesus, **tired** as He was from the journey, sat thus down by the well. It was about the sixth hour." Touching description! He had been traversing as already described in the introductory chapter, during the long hours of morning, the valleys of Ephraim, on His way to the Wady El-Mokhna, and then along the unsheltered plain itself, under the blaze of that Syrian sun.

The ordinary mealtime of noon had arrived, when hunger was superadded to physical fatigue, and being weary with His journey and long fast, He "sat down by the well." This is an expression which, indefinite in itself, has received various interpretations. By some it has been supposed to mean that He sat there 'as best He could;' either on the hard parapet, or else on the beaten ground, making the rough curb-stone a pillow for His head. By others, and among these Chrysostom, that He flung Himself down 'as soon as He could,' upon the first seat He could find. Others, connecting the word "thus" with the word "tired," refer it to His weary position; He sat "thus"—faint, toilworn—His hand, perhaps, on His throbbing temples, shielding His head from the oppressive sun-rays. Whichever meaning we adopt, here at least, we have an apparently poor pilgrim of Galilee, companionless, hungry, thirsty, prostrated with fatigue, thankful, as we shall find, of a cup of water from a wayside well, but being unprovided with rope or pitcher or other appliance, compelled to wait for some chance visitor to supply the boon.

It is in such incidental occurrences that our Lord's humanity and the lowliness of His humiliation are most touchingly exemplified. We have other more marked and expressive illustrations of His weakness and weariness—His participation alike in the sufferings and innocent infirmities of the race He came to save. As when, amid the peculiar white limestone deserts which overhang the Dead Sea, utterly devoid of sustenance for man and beast, the arch-enemy assaulted Him through one of the avenues of our physical nature, and, on the plea of demonstrating His divinity, would make Him yield to the temptation of converting the rocks around into bread, to stay the race of hunger. Or as, after a long day's unremitting labor on the shores of the Lake of Galilee, overtasked nature asserted her claims, and on the rough planks of a fishing-boat He lay fast asleep. Or when, in the lingering agonies of the Cross, His life-blood ebbing away, He gasped forth with fevered burning lips, "I thirst."

But, we repeat, it is in the quieter nooks of that valley of humiliation which He trod, that we come often on the most affecting of such testimonies. As when His poverty is attested by His virgin mother, eight days after His birth, "when the time of her purification according to the law had been completed," unable to bring the customary sacrifice of "a lamb for a burnt-offering," she resorts to the gracious alternative provided for the *poor* of the people—"a pair of turtle doves and two young pigeons." Or when He has to summon a fish from the sea of Gennesaret to pay the tribute-debt

He is otherwise *unable to pay*. Or when mind and body together shattered by the news of the beloved Baptist's cruel death, He has to suspend His labors; and seek the restorative for a wounded spirit in rest and solitude. Or in crossing Mount Olivet, when it is touchingly said, "Early in the morning as He was on His way back to the city He was hungry;" and when that bodily hunger was mocked by the pretentious leaves of a fig tree "where He found no fruit." Or when, on His way to Calvary, the agonizing strain of the preceding day and night, alike on His physical and moral nature, caused Him to fall powerless under the weight of His cross.

Or yet again, as here, when we behold Him a weary, exhausted wayfarer on the Palestine highway, the sun of high noon beating on His unsheltered head, *asking a cup of cold water from the poor sinner He was about to pluck as a brand from the burning!* It has often been noted, that though from time to time He exercised miraculous powers to provide for the needs and even the redundancies of others, (as in the case of the wine at Cana, or the bread and fishes at Bethsaida-Julias,) He never called these into requisition for *Himself*.

At this very moment, how easily could He, to whom belonged the cattle on a thousand hills and every bird that soared among these surrounding valleys, have summoned from the groves of Shechem and Gerizim winged messengers like those which fed of old His great prophet, to minister to His necessities. No, He had only to speak the word, and nobler ministering spirits—legions of angels—would have trooped to His side with the bread of heaven—the best fruits culled from the celestial paradise. But "in all things it behooved Him to be like His brethren." He had chosen poverty as His birthright; and *His divine prerogatives, so far as regarded Himself, are never employed to mitigate the needs and woes and privations of the estate to which He thus voluntarily submitted.* Even on the cross He refused the soporific offered to deaden the acuteness of pain. And now, faint and weary at the well of Sychar, He is content with the draught of water, until His disciples return from their errand to the adjoining city "to buy food."

Oh most precious and consolatory truth! That Savior to whom I owe my everlasting salvation, is the Brother of my nature—in all points tempted like as I am. It is impressively said regarding Him by the great apostle, "He took not on Him the nature of angels, but He took on Him the seed of Abraham," (Heb. 2:16.) In other words, it was not the *Angelic*, but the *Adamic* nature he given to assume. Why not the angelic? why not the nobler nature of these principalities and powers—the chieftains and aristocracy of God's family? We answer, for two reasons: first, The angelic nature is a spiritual essence. "A spirit has not flesh and bones:" it is incapable, therefore, of corporeal suffering. It behooved Him as the divine oblation to suffer, and to suffer in the nature—the *human* nature which had sinned. "Therefore," says the apostle, adverting to this very point, "we see Jesus made a little lower than the angels *for the suffering of death.*" And then, secondly, in addition to this, and more especially—had the assumption of the angelic nature been otherwise compatible with the requirements of the divine law, it would have prevented participation in feeling and sympathy with the myriads He came to redeem. An angel can sympathize only with his brother angel—the brotherhood of ministering spirits. It requires a *man* to sympathize with his brother man. But *we have* SUCH a Brother—such a High Priest "touched with the feeling of our infirmities."

Moreover, while He had it in His power to select from all the degrees and gradations of society—the mass of the human family being composed of the lowly and the poor, the children of need and poverty and suffering, He *has forever sanctified and dignified POVERTY by taking it as His earthly inheritance.* And thus, while those occupying the pinnacles of worldly greatness—while widowed royalty on the throne can cling to Him in this blessed identity of humanity as the Prince of sufferers, preeminently can the widow and orphan of the mine, and the hut, and the lonely garret—the teeming thousands struggling with hard toil and privation and poverty, claim the exalted sympathy of Him who, "though He was rich, yet for their sakes became poor."

But it would be a poor and insufficient anchorage for the human soul, in its deathless interests, if this were all. However pure and untainted that HUMANITY was, however wide and comprehensive in its sympathies, we require something else, something more stable to lean upon, than the mere virtues of a spotless human life—the ideal of a perfect manhood nature. Blessed be God, the might of DEITY is revealed in conjunction with the tenderness of Humanity, "His name is Immanuel, God with us."

And it is remarkable how often, how generally, the two natures in the one Person are associated, alike in typical prefiguration, in gospel narrative, and in dogmatic statement. The modern Socinian or Unitarian overlooks or ignores this. He takes the *coin* and gazes only on the side bearing the human mark and superscription—the manger, the temptation, the unsullied life, the hero-death: he has not turned to the reverse golden side, gleaming with divine attestations. He goes to the old Sinai wilderness, where that same Savior, the covenant angel, revealed Himself as the deliverer of typical Israel; but he sees only a bush—a desert shrub, "a root out of a dry ground," burning with fire—the emblem of lowly, yet pure humanity: he has failed to hear the voice emanating from that oracle of burning flame, "I AM THAT I AM!" "I am the Lord God of your fathers, the GOD of Abraham, the GOD of Isaac, and the GOD of Jacob." He goes to the gospel story. He beholds a lowly individual baptized in the Jordan, receiving a sinner's lowly rite; but he fails to see that "fulfillment of all righteousness" transfigured into a divine manifesto, by the opened heavens and the descending dove and the witnessing voice. He beholds a slumbering man breathing heavily on the deck of a Tiberias fishing boat; but he fails to hear Him rebuking, with the voice of omnipotence, the winds and waves. He beholds the expiring criminal on Calvary, thorn-crowned, scourged, naked, buffeted—a pure and innocent, but a helpless, powerless martyr, dragged to unmerited death; but he fails to note how that mysterious Sufferer evokes a tribute from the dumb earth as it trembles to support His ignominious cross— the upheaving rocks around resenting the insults to the great Lord of all. And here, while he beholds an exhausted traveler reclining on the parapet of the well at Sychar, he forgets the omniscient glance which could unlock the deep secrets of the heart which quailed under the eye of Infinite purity, and the tongue which "told her all things that she ever did."

It is the same with regard to the dogmatic and doctrinal assertions of evangelists and apostles. The Unitarian sees proof positive of the humanity of Christ in John's unequivocal assertion, "The Word was made flesh;" but he has failed to mark the antecedent announcement, equally unequivocal, in the same page, "The Word was God." He reads the unchallenged statement of Paul in the commencement of his Epistle to the Hebrews, "You are my Son, this day have I begotten You;" but he has omitted the counterpart assertion, "Your throne, *O God*, is forever and ever." He reads in the declaration of the same apostle, the undoubted testimony to the lowly humanity assumed—"He made Himself of no reputation, and took upon Him the form of a servant, and was made in the likeness of men;" but he has eliminated from his creed and his proof the opening words, "Who being in the form of God, thought it not robbery to be equal with God." He reads in connection with the noble pedigree of Israel, "Of whom, as concerning the flesh,

Christ came;" but he fails to finish the sentence, "who is over all, God blessed forever," (Rom. 9:5.) He looks to Christ as an example. He owns it to be the noblest, purest, loftiest, of restored and regenerated humanity; and he reads in the Epistle to the Colossians, "As you have therefore received Christ Jesus the Lord, so walk in Him;" but he has culpably concealed and overlooked that lofty introduction in the same epistle, "Who is the image of the invisible God, the firstborn of every creature: for by Him were all things created that are in heaven, and that are in earth, visible and invisible, whether they be thrones, or dominions, or principalities, or powers; all things were created by Him, and for Him; and He is before all things, and by Him all things consist. In Him dwells all the fullness of the Godhead bodily," (Col. 1:15-17; 2:6, 9.)

Reader, be it yours to rejoice in the glorious *combination*; that He who orders the magnificent marchings of Pleiades and Orion, who guides Arcturus with his sons—took into union with the might and majesty of Deity, the lowliness and the weakness of suffering humanity; that He who had the borrowed manger at Bethlehem, and led the youth of artisan toil at Nazareth, and sat the fainting pilgrim by the well of Jacob, can enter not only into the deeper and nobler sympathies of our nature, but even into its lowliest necessities and poorest, lowliest needs—hunger and thirst and faintness and lassitude—so that we may cease to wonder that many a soiled leaf has been doubled down by the begrimed fingers of the children of poverty, at the fourth chapter of John's Gospel.

May it not have been this which induced the very beggars on the streets and highways of Palestine, when they heard that "Jesus of Nazareth passed by," to cry out, "Jesus, Son of David, have mercy upon us!"

And He wears that humanity now. He is changed indeed in His outward estate. The wayfarer of Shechem is enthroned as King of saints amid a multitude which no man can number. But it is not the less true that the Divine Shepherd, who is now leading His flock to the living fountains of waters in heaven, is, in the sympathies of His glorified manhood, the unchanged Savior, who sat by the fountain on earth. When the loud wail of suffering humanity is borne to His ear, it gets the response of a *Human heart*. That noontide hour of Sychar is in habitual remembrance with Him, to whom a thousand years are as one day, for He is "Jesus Christ, the same yesterday, and today, and forever!"

Are there any whose eyes trace these pages, who, like Him, are weary—weary in another sense—weary with life's journey, the sun of TRIAL beating on their unsheltered heads; weary with pain, weary with heart sorrows—the disciples gone away—left companionless and alone; that too at the noontide hour, the hour they most needed rest and refreshment an d comfort? "Consider Him . . . *so that you will not grow weary and lose heart.*" Go seat yourselves by that weary One, and hear Him whisper in your ears, in the midst of His own languor and faintness, "I know your sorrows!"

Are others weary, but, not like Him, weary with SIN? who have come up through these hot valleys of temptation, and are now sitting by the poisoned wells of existence, the pitcher broken at the cistern; nothing to draw with; the zest of life gone; the hot sun blazing in the meridian; no canopy, no fig tree shade, no rocky shelter to screen them from the fierce rays? Go, seat yourselves, too, by that weary One. Like the bird long struggling with baffled wings against the storm, drop into the crevices of this true Rock and hear the word of welcome, 'Come to Me, and I will give you rest.'

Are there others again—how many such are there—who have reached that period of existence which reminds them of Sychar's noontide—who are undergoing the burden and heat of the day in the very midst of life's arduous callings. Manhood's sixth hour; manhood in its prime! It is a befitting pausing place and pausing season in the journey, a blessed opportunity to seat yourselves by the well and the water of life. "About the sixth hour." One half of existence over. The morning and early hours gone. The steep valleys of early manhood, with their climbing struggles, their "hill difficulties," surmounted. But still, who that has been most successful in the past half journey—who that has reached life's midway well with least toiling effort—but has to fling himself down and confess that he is 'weary,' and if the living water be yet untasted, to cry out, in the anguish of unquenched and unsatisfied longings, "*I thirst.*" Half way!

Oh, with many, with most, it is past the half-way journey. They have seen that sun, which has now attained its zenith, rise; but they are not to see it set. The valley of death, like the valley of Shechem, may be close at hand, its entrance within sight, while the true fountain of life is still unrepaired to.

My brother, as with the pilgrim in the caravan of old, or the traveler at this day by the Well of Jacob, you are seated in a spiritual sense there, gazing either on the Ebal of curses, or the Gerizim of blessings. Which are you to choose? to go on and brave the entrance under Ebal's frowning rocks; or to drink the living, life-giving water, and begin forthwith the ascent of the true Mountain of beatitudes beyond the Valley of the shadow? Is it the Sabbath's reposeful noontide hour which you are now enjoying; in which you are invited to turn aside and "rest a while," after traversing the week's rough highways of toil—to take off the dust-covered sandals and be alone with Jesus? Convert the hour of rest into the hour of solemn meditation and prayerful resolve. Look upwards to these mountain summits which enclose the valley. Select your alternative. Behold there is set before you the blessing and the curse, (Deut. 11:26.) "Who may ascend the hill of the Lord? Who may stand in His holy place? He who has clean hands and a pure heart: who does not lift up his soul to an idol, or swear by what is false." He shall receive THE BLESSING from the Lord, and righteousness from the God of his salvation."

"THE DRAWER OF WATER"

When a Samaritan woman came to draw water, Jesus said to her, "Will you give Me a drink?" John 4:7

In the previous chapter we contemplated the Divine Pilgrim, wearied from His journey, seated by the well of Jacob. Let us turn for a little to the other visitant, at that consecrated spot, who divides with Him the interest of the narrative: "A Samaritan woman came to draw water."

The first question which naturally suggests itself is, *What brought her there?* And the question is all the more pertinent to those who are familiar with the locality. The well of Jacob, as has been previously noted, is at a considerable distance from the modern Nablous. Indeed, if the ancient Sychar be identical with the present Shechem, it cannot be less than a mile and a half. At all events, much nearer her home were two copious fountains, Ain Defileh and Ain Balata, which must have been as old as the days of the Canaanites, besides innumerable springs within and around the city; and whatever else may have been the changes which eighteen centuries have produced, we may feel assured that the number of the wells and streams of ancient times can have undergone no diminution. There must have been, therefore, some special reason to induce this female of Sychar, in the heat of noontide, to take an otherwise superfluous and unnecessary journey to a well that is specially designated as *"deep"* and the drawing from which must have been accompanied with considerable manual labor. The very hour, too, was unusual and peculiar. Of old, and to this day, evening was the time at which the wells and cisterns of Palestine were surrounded with living throngs. It is only the chance wayfarer or passing caravan that are found pausing at noon for refreshment. Moreover, as has been observed by Dr. Robinson, "that is was not the public well of the city is probable from the circumstance, noted in verse 11, that there was here no public accommodation for drawing water."

The answer which we think is, on the whole, most satisfactory, is the one suggested by the same learned writer and followed by others, that it was more than likely *a peculiar value* set on the water—a superstitious virtue supposed to attach to the old patriarch's well—which induced this woman to protract her journey and brave the midday heat. In various parts of Europe, *superstition* has reared its convent, monastery or shrine around reputed *sacred fountains* which have borne for ages the name of their founder or patron saint, and been credited with an inherent charm for the cure of diseases alike physical and spiritual. What must have been the sanctity which, in the Jewish age, gathered round these holy relics of Israel's Pilgrim fathers at Beersheba and Sychar! no mythical saints of a mythical calendar, but the veritable spots where the tent and altar of the Friend of God and of His children's children were pitched, where the smoke of their offering ascended, and the rites of patriarchal hospitality were dispensed.

An objection, however, to this surmise may reasonably occur. We can quite imagine such a motive (we could not denounce it as superstitious, we would, to a certain extent, rather commend it as hallowed) actuating a true child of Abraham and Jacob—a partaker of their faith; but we can scarcely imagine a profligate and degenerate descendant of these holy patriarchs making any such nice discriminating distinction between the distant ancestral well and one of the gushing fountains that sang its way in the valley close by her own home.

This objection would be tenable, were it not for a strange peculiarity, in this composite fallen nature of ours, by which *cringing superstition is not infrequently found allied with licentiousness.* It has been well observed, "There is a kind of 'religious' *feeling* (often possessed by people of a susceptible and emotional temperament) which, where moral principle is lacking, gives birth at once to a sensuous superstition and a sensuous life." In the most abandoned heart there is always something to utter a protest against its sin; and along with this, some *false refuge* or expedient to shake off the uneasy feeling of guilt and of abused and violated responsibility. As, at times, amid the wrecks of the old ruin tangled and matted with rank weed and nettle—crumbling in decay, may be discovered the piece of now marred, but once delicate sculpture, indicating and memorializing its vanished glory—so even in the soul which is a moral wreck, there is found, now and then, in the midst of its fallen capitals and moldering walls, some strange indices, so to speak, of the tracery of a diviner than human finger "on the plaster of the wall" of that once kingly palace.

In the case of some, this manifests itself in a groping after higher life and truer verities. With others, as with the Samaritan woman, it is no more than a dim recognition of that moral responsibility of which we have just spoken, coupled with *an undefined mysterious dread of divine retribution*; but taking the *counterfeit form of seeking to atone for inner heart impurity by the performance of some outer act of religiousness.* In one word, counterbalancing the *life of guilt,* and quieting the stings and rebukes of conscience by the penance and the pilgrimage—giving the fruit of the body, or the toil of the body, for the sin of the soul.

We see it in the case of the *Mohammedan,* reveling in all that is morally debasing, yet saving the pittances of a lifetime and braving weeks and months of perilous endurance to accomplish his pilgrimage to Mecca. We see it in the case of the *Roman Catholic*: for in what but this consists one of the fatal charms of Romanism and of the semi-Romanism of the day, whose essence is contained in what is called 'sacramental efficacy;' and where *the mere external act of worship,* is made a counterbalance for the worldly or abandoned life. Such is frail, inconsistent, fallen human nature; and this too, we may add, not alone in the case of the gentle Hindu, or the sensual Mussulman, or the superstitious Romanist, or the mediaeval Ritualist; but under every phase of religion, not excepting the nominal Protestant and Puritan, *where that religion is a mere form,* not a regenerating power.

The woman of Samaria is thus the type and representative of a by no means limited class, among whom depravity of character is found associated either with *silly superstition* or with *hollow sanctimoniousness*; a degraded citizen of Sychar, yet going at times with meditative step, and in the pride of sect and of religious ancestry, to the "Holy Well," and thereby, in spite of a life of unblushing sin, thinking she was doing the God of Jacob service! Oh, the human heart, like that well of Jacob, is "deep"—deep in its corruptions, deep in its self-deceptions. "The heart is deceitful above all things and desperately wicked, who can know it?"

But to pass to one other more practical reflection—the *Guiding hand* which brought the woman of Samaria at that particular time to draw water. We shall afterwards come to read in her brief biography a wondrous chapter in the *volume of Grace:* but we have here to mark a preliminary page in *the book of Providence.*

Nothing, in the earthly sense of the word, was more purely accidental, than the going of this citizen of Sychar that day to the well at sultry noontide. She left her home with no thought but to bring in her pitcher a draught from the well-known fountain. Never dreamt she for a moment of an undesigned meeting that was to shape, and mold, and recast her whole future. Had she come there a day sooner, or at the usual evening time for the drawing of water, amid the hum of voices and the bleating of flocks, she would have missed that "still hour" of divine musing and heavenly communion: she would have returned the heathen and reprobate she had gone. But there is a directing, controlling, superintending Power guiding all human plans and purposes, "rough hew them as we will."

Who can doubt that, *all unknown and unforeseen by her, it was one of those ordinary everyday providences of God*, included in the supervision "of all His creatures and all their actions," which we are compelled implicitly to believe, if we would unriddle and understand the mystery of the world. Make that journey to the well a mere happy accident—a curious and singular coincidence in which there was no divine foreknowledge and decree, and as a matter of course we write "chance" on the momentous results to which the meeting led—the founding and extension of that Church which sprang from the woman of Samaria as its nursing mother. If we stop short of the only true solution of that journey, as being one of the eternal purposes of the Most High—prearranged and predetermined by Him—we virtually dissever God from history. Accident! Chance! No; the name of that woman was written in the Book of life. The same "needs be" of the divine 'determinate counsel' which brought the Redeemer there, brought also her, who, before that noontide sun sank behind Gerizim, was to He made a trophy of His grace.

Indeed we cannot speak of such apparently trivial occurrences as "accidents" without virtually dethroning Deity, wresting the sovereignty of His own world from the hands of the Supreme. The peradventures and contingencies of men are the interpreters of His will, the executioners of His purposes, heralds sent forth to fulfill His high behests. If we deny particular providences, we must deny more special ones. *If we deny God's hand in the minute events of daily life, we must, to be consistent, eliminate His overruling power in the rise and fall of empires.* Minute occurrences, apparently the most trifling, have not infrequently involved the destinies of nations, and the blessing or curse of generations unborn.

Every schoolboy knows the authenticated fact in our own early Scottish history, how the fate of this kingdom hung, so to speak, on a spider's web; how the success of that tiny insect nerved the arm of her chieftain kin—as like himself, six times baffled, it reached on a seventh effort the rafters above his head—roused him from his couch of despondency and led to the victory which secured his country's independence. By refusing to recognize God's direct overruling providence in an incident so trifling, we must, as a matter of course, sever from His cognizance and supervision every subsequent historic event in our nation's annals to which that apparently trivial accident gave birth.

The reader of "The Rise and Fall of the Roman Empire" may remember a similar story with a lesson: the passage wherein the skeptic writer, in the pomp of stately history, tells of the little bird of the desert which rose from the mouth of the cave, where Mahomet, the false prophet, had taken refuge from his pursuers, and by which occurrence he evaded certain death. He records, with a covert skeptic's sneer, (what the Christian may read as a great truth) that "the flight of that bird changed the destinies of the world." Yes! this is true, 'but not as the infidel would represent it—as if that winged tenant of the wilderness had usurped the place of the Great Supreme. We accept his saying, but it is with the interpretation that the almighty Ruler, the God of providence, had set that tiny warder by the cave's mouth, prepared its perch by the rugged entrance, and gave the summons to fly.

Deny God's providence as extending to so minute and trifling an occurrence, and you wrest from Him the cognizance and foreknowledge of the vast influence which that impostor was yet to exercise on the world's history. In other words, you admit the 'heathen deity of chance' into your Parthenon; you fling the reins on the coursers' necks and surrender all idea of Divine control—resolving all history into a fortuitous concurrence of chances, just as the infidel world-maker would resolve all this fair creation, with its harmonious movements and nicely adjusted machinery, into the old fortuitous concurrence of atoms. *No, no; man proposes, but God disposes. He who wheels the planets in their courses, marks the sparrow's fall.* He who swept Babylon with the broom of destruction, or overthrew Pharaoh in the Red Sea, or raised up the princely Cyrus to be the deliverer of His people, conducted that female's steps that day, at the noontide hour, to Sychar's well. He who brought (in similar circumstances) Rebekah, Rachel, and Zipporah to other eastern fountains to be wedded to the princely fathers of the Hebrew people, brought their descendant to nobler and more glorious spiritual espousals—to pledge her troth to the Divine Redeemer, who was soon to ratify these espousals by the outpouring of His precious blood, and proclaim to a whole outcast world, "Your Maker is your husband, the Lord of Hosts is His name."

We see every day the same truth illustrated in our own individual histories. Events, often apparently trivial and unimportant— what the world calls accidents, form really and truly the mighty levers of life, altering and revolutionizing our whole future. The relationships of earth, the spheres of our labor, the connections of business, the bounds of our habitation, are all in one sense accidental. The merest trifles have touched the springs of action; a twig or stone has altered the direction of life's footpath; the jutting rock in the stream has altered its course in the valley; the casual meeting of a friend on the street may have led to the most important crisis in our history: the youth on the verge of sin and ruin by stumbling accidentally into some house of God, has been led to hear the word, which to him now is like the memory of that well of Sychar to the saved penitent of Samaria—associated with living streams and everlasting life.

Let us rejoice in the simple but sublime assurance that all that happens is ordered for us—that the vessel in which we sail is not like the abandoned ship of the great painter—a deserted log in the wild waters, without helm or mast or compass, driven here and there by the capricious breath of the tempest—but that rather, like the gigantic wheels in Ezekiel's vision, the wheel within wheel is propelled by Omnipotence. Better still, as in the same vision the prophet of Chebar saw "above the firmament the likeness of a throne, as the appearance of a sapphire stone, and upon the likeness of the throne was the likeness as the appearance of a man above upon it;" so it is for us to know, and to rejoice in the knowledge, that every event is in the hands of the Savior who died for us, and who has given us this mightiest proof and pledge of dying love, that all things (even the most mysterious) are working together for our good.

Oh, even over our bitterest trials let us write the gleaming words, *"He had to go."* Blessed for us if that "had to" result—as it did in the case of the Lord of pilgrims and the repentant sinner, in bringing us to the well's mouth, to hold close converse on the all-momentous question of our salvation, and in the thirst of the world's sultry noon to get our parched souls filled with the water of salvation. Meanwhile be this our prayer, "Show me Your ways, O Lord, teach me Your paths;" "Lead me in Your truth and teach me;" "Lead me in the way everlasting!" Whether it be amid the groves and singing streams and sunshine of Gerizim, or amid the "blackness and darkness and tempest" of Ebal, I will hear the guiding voice saying, "Follow Me. This is the way, walk in it."

"Lead, kindly Light; amid the encircling gloom
Lead me on:
The night is dark, and I am far from home,
Lead me on.
Keep my feet, I do not ask to see
The distant scene; one step enough for me.

"I was not ever thus, nor prayed that You
Should lead me on;
I loved to choose and see my path, but now
Lead me on.
I loved the glare of day, and, spite of fears,
Pride ruled my will: remember not past years.

"So long Your power has blest me, sure it still
Will lead me on,
Over valley and hill, through stream and torrent, until
The night is gone;
And, with the morn, those angel faces smile
Which I have loved long since, and lost awhile."

THE CONFERENCE

When a Samaritan woman came to draw water, Jesus said to her, "Will you give Me a drink?" John 4:7

The meeting and conference here unfolded to us with the woman of Samaria, is a graphic representation of what has occurred thousand thousand times since; when the soul is brought into real, though invisible communion with the Savior. Other moments of our individual histories may be solemn and momentous, and vast worldly issues dependent upon them; but none to compare with this. It is death coming in contact with life—the mortal with the immortal—the finite with the infinite—time with eternity—dust with Deity—the sinner with the great God. What an impressive, mysterious contrast, between those two who now met for the first time by the well of the patriarch! Frowning, lightning-scathed, storm-wreathed Ebal was confronting close by, the smiling groves and sunshine of Gerizim: but what a feeble type and image of these living beings standing face to face: impurity confronting spotless purity: a lost and ruined soul confronting its holy, yet forgiving Redeemer. It is the gospel in expressive parable.

This prodigal daughter is a striking counterpart of the prodigal son in our Lord's touching discourse. Like him, she had wandered from her father's house. In all riotous living she had reveled. She had probably at that moment around her head and neck and arms, what we have seen often and again adorning the females at the wells of Palestine, strings of coins, or, it may be, jewels, (in her case the mementos and rewards of sin.) But this glittering outer tinsel screened moral beggary and misery within. She had been feeding on the garbage of the wilderness; and her inarticulate cry was the echo of his wild plaint, "I perish with hunger!" May we not imagine her in her hours of deep remorse, (for who, the most degraded and reprobate, have not these?) brought up as she must have been in the knowledge of the God of Abraham, and Isaac, and Jacob—may we not imagine her saying at times within herself, "I will arise and go to my Father"? We do not say that any such definite religious longing or aspiration now brought her to the Well: far from it. As we shall afterwards find, though it may have been partly dissembled, she affected rather the contrary—lightness of heart and levity of speech, to the unknown stranger. But that she *had* her seasons of deep soul misery and self-reproach cannot be doubted; and coming as she now did, with a superstitious feeling at least to the fountain of the patriarch, she would be so far tutored and prepared, by her approach to that holy ground, for the unexpected converse which awaited her there.

At all events, if this prodigal had at the moment no thoughts of her *Father;* her Father—her Savior—her Brother—her Friend, had gracious thoughts of *her.* He "saw her afar off and had compassion upon her." He stripped the meretricious jewels off her head, and put the ring of His own adopting love on her ringless finger, and the sandals of a peace she had never known before, on her feet. Yes, and so great was His joy at finding the long-lost one, that when the disciples came afterwards from the city to their weary, hunger-stricken Master with the purchased bread, and with the request, "Master, eat;" we believe, for very joy, He could not look at the provided earthly refreshment. "I have food to eat," says He, which the world knows not of"—"This my sister, my prodigal child, was dead and is alive again; she was lost and is found!"

In adverting, in the present chapter, to some preliminary features of this conference, we would remark *How the Lord Jesus, in His dealings with His people, adapts Himself to their peculiar character and circumstances and necessities.*

This is specially illustrated in the narrative of the woman of Samaria, from its juxtaposition in John's Gospel with another recorded interview of a similar kind—that with Nicodemus. In the one case, Christ had to bear with a proud Pharisee, a member of the Jewish Sanhedrin, one at whose door probably could be laid no glaring sin—a man scrupulous in external decencies, "as touching the righteousness which is of the Law, blameless." Moreover, in the character of this inquirer there was a constitutional timidity which is manifest even in the subsequent avowal of his discipleship. Though he brings costly offerings of his affection and love for the embalming of his Lord's body, he does not share the bolder moral courage of his Arimathean brother, in demanding from Pilate the sacred treasure. Jesus accordingly deals tenderly and sensitively with him, as one who is the prey of that "fear of man which brings a snare." He meets his case and its difficulties. He will not wound either his pride or his fears by challenging him to converse in broad day; but He will open for him His silent oratory on Olivet. He will permit him and encourage him to steal there, night by night, to unburden the doubts and misgivings of his anxious, thoughtful, truth-seeking, candid soul. He who suits the soldier to his place, and the place to the soldier, who "tempers the wind to the shorn lamb," will not break this bruised reed nor quench this smoking, flax, until He bring forth judgment unto victory. *"The same came to Jesus by night."*

In dealing with the woman of Samaria, again, with her bold spirit and blunted feelings, there were no such tender scruples to consult; there was rather a propriety in holding converse with this impure child of darkness in the blaze of day. *She* needed the piercing blast of the north wind, bringing with it sharp convictions of sin; barbed arrow after arrow was sent through the folds of guilt covering her heart, until that heart lay broken and bleeding at the feet of her Divine Restorer—while the other, requiring rather the south wind of tender consolation and comfort, was led step by step, from the necessity of "the new birth," up to the sublime unfoldings of the love of God in the free gift of His Son and the bestowal of everlasting life. The two form a living commentary on the prophet's description of the Almighty's dealings, "In measure, when it shoots forth, you will debate with it; He stays His rough wind in the day of His east wind."

We may gather another affecting and impressive thought from these two conjoined, yet contrasted cases. They together recall the truth, already referred to in a preceding chapter, but here brought before us under a fresh illustration—*the unresting love which, while on earth, Christ had for sinners:* that any personal sacrifices He would make, any personal deprivation He would endure, to save a soul from death, and to hide a multitude of sins.

In the case of Nicodemus, night by night Jesus willingly surrendered or cut short His needed rest, that He might calm the perturbations of one agitated spirit. He would not give sleep to His eyes, nor slumber to His eyelids, until in that man's heart He found a place for the Lord, a habitation for the mighty God of Jacob. And in the interview with the Samaritan woman, as we have seen, the hour of greatest recorded bodily weariness is with equal willingness alienated from rest, that He may bring the wanderer to His fold. We have watched the Great Shepherd of the sheep just terminating a long and fatiguing bodily journey through the hot valleys of Ephraim. But a soul is to be saved. He suspends needed repose from toil; and, as it were, with staff in hand, resumes the journey over rock and hedge and tangled precipice, in order that when His absent disciples return from their errand to the neighboring, city, He may call together these His friends and neighbors, saying to them, "Rejoice with me, for I have found my sheep which was lost." Here is the true covenant Angel who wrestled with Jacob at the brook Jabbok. "He wrestled," we read, "all night with him until the breaking of the day." But when day broke, did the wrestlings of that mysterious visitant terminate with the experience of that solitary man in the gorges of Jordan? No; daybreak is only a new summons for fresh efforts and deeds of love. Some new case requires His presence; some other pilgrim by some other brook, at that early morn, demands His aid and support. "Let Me go," He says, "for the day breaks." Immediately He takes His departure. Leaving the patriarch with a new and significant name, the badge at once of blessing and victory, He speeds His way—on, still on— saying, to this soul and that in His untiring flight, "O Israel, you have destroyed yourself, but in Me is your help!"

Another and different thought suggests itself in connection with the interview at Jacob's well. It is, that *this conference of Christ, the most minutely detailed conference of the Bible, was with a Woman.*

This strikes us comparatively little in our land of gospel privilege; because, females have been exalted by Christianity, and Christianity's founder, to the place they were designed by their Creator to occupy. There is nothing to us strange or unusual in a woman taking part in a conference about divine things. On the contrary, it is females who now throng our religious meetings, and are the best and most effective auxiliaries in every department of practical Christian effort. But it must be remembered it was far different among the Hebrews. The same social degradation which characterized the female sex amid pagan nations, and which is the curse of Orientalism at this moment, was so far at least, and especially in the age to which we refer, grafted on Judaism. "The Rabbis forbade her instruction, deemed her incapable of it; first made her despicable, and then despised her." Even the disciples, those whom we might have thought had already been taught the creed of a nobler Christian chivalry, "marveled that He talked with *the woman*," (ver. 27.) It was a violation of their conventional ideas talking to her at all; above all, talking to her about religious themes, the soul, "the gift of God," "everlasting life."

But has not Christ, by this very conversation and interview, inaugurated a new era and warrant for the spiritual activities of woman: not only conversing with her about her own soul, but sending her forth a herald of salvation to her fellow-townsmen, and making the Church of Samaria imperishably identified with her name and labors? To all of us, therefore, that hour of converse has its sacred—with many, the most sacred memories of life. Jesus consecrating this female's mission was, in one sense, consecrating the mission of every mother as she bends over her infant's cradle, or as she gathers her children around her knee and tells them of the great salvation.

Yes, if there was one thing more than another that made Christianity stand out in bold and beautiful contrast with the debasing and sensual creed of heathenism, it was when the adorable Redeemer removed the swathing bands and fetters from the body and soul of woman, and sent her forth from her couch of degradation, earth's ministering angel, "walking and leaping and praising God." Where would have been the noblest and the best names in the Church's annals, had female influence, had a mother's tongue, been gagged, and a mother's prayers been stifled? Where would have been our Augustines and our Origens, our Zwingles and Luthers, our Watts and Bunyans, if Christ had not stood by His vacant sepulcher in the morning of His resurrection, and asking the question before an enslaving world, "Woman, why are you weeping?" dried her tears, elevated her nature, refined her sympathies, vindicated her rights, redressed her wrongs, burst her bonds and set her free!

That hour and that conversation at Sychar were the first-fruits of a glorious harvest—a prophecy and pledge of unnumbered blessings, which many a pious son has to thank God for; yes, over which many a prodigal has to rejoice through the burning tears of a dying but penitent hour. John Newton, in that dark night at the helm of his vessel, would not have remembered the hymn which his mother taught him, and which revolutionized his life, but for the new charter which Christ put into the hands of the woman of Samaria, and such as she.

And with the same reference, let us read in the touching story also a prophecy of the future; not as to what Christianity has done for us and for Christendom, but what the power of Christianity will yet do for those down-trodden lands where that new and glorious charter was first written, and where woman is still the soulless drudge, the grinding slave of unnatural oppression. In no part of Palestine more so than near and around this very spot where Christ spoke these wondrous words at Jacob's well, is woman overtasked and degraded—toil her cruel birthright; her dwelling is not on the sunlit slopes of Gerizim, but amid the frowning curses of Ebal. The cross has waned and the crescent is triumphant. Since the light of the Christianity of early apostolic days has there been extinguished—the sacred name of its Founder become a reproach and a scorn—well may the wailing words of the noblest in the early band of Jewish females be echoed by her oppressed successors, "They have taken away my Lord, and I know not where they have laid Him!" But the day of emancipation is at hand. What Christianity has done for us, it will yet do for those sitting under the shadow of death.

It is remarkable that in many of the inspired prefigurations of Israel's glowing future in the millennial era, the equality of woman is a specified feature and characteristic, "My sons shall come from far, my *daughters* shall be nursed at my side." "Bring my sons from far, and my *daughters* from the ends of the earth." Who can forget that it was a woman, a Jewish woman, who was last at the cross and first at the grave? Who can forget that it was the women of the early Church whose devotion and moral heroism evoked Paul's warmest benedictions and salutations—Phoebe, Priscilla, Junia, Tryphena, Tryphosa, and others in the honored sisterhood of the faith. So, may we not expect, as one of the bright features in the ingathering of regenerated Israel that woman, Christianized, and, by being Christianized, dignified, elevated, and refined, will prove, like this female of Sychar, a herald of glad tidings—the gentle dove of peace sent forth with the olive-branch from the true ark of God. In that lofty Hebrew Alleluia, which is to blend with the Gentile Hosanna in welcoming in the King of the Jews to His throne on Mount Zion—the metropolis of a millennial earth—loud amid timbrel and harp will be the voices of the Miriams and the Deborahs, who, in higher strains than on the Red Sea, or amid the hills of Kedesh, will "sing the song of Moses, the servant of God, and the song of the Lamb," and help to carry the glad strain from home to home, from valley to valley, from city to city, until the whole land will send up the shout, loud as the sound of many waters, "Blessed is He who comes in the name of the Lord!" "Rejoice, O *daughter* of Zion; behold, your King comes to you!" "Loose yourself from the bands of your neck, O captive daughter of Zion." You may now be like the bird with broken wing—a caged captive, unable to sing the Lord's song in a strange land. But the day is at hand when the Gospel's soaring pinion of life and liberty will be yours again; when "you shall be as a dove whose wings are covered with silver, and her feathers with yellow gold."

While we are permitted thus joyfully to remember, that in Christ there is neither Jew nor Greek, barbarian, Scythian, bond nor free, "male nor *female*;" the great practical question for each of us as individuals, is not what the religion of Christ has done for the world in the past, or may yet do in the world of the future, but *what has that religion done for me?* Do *we* know anything of the converting and regenerating power which plucked that degraded Samaritan as a jewel from the crown of the prince of darkness, to irradiate the brow of Jesus? What *grace* can do, in changing and transforming the worst and most hopeless; quickening those who are dead; and animating the groveling spirit with new motives, new principles, new tastes, new feelings, new aspirations! That very patriarch at whose well she stood, was himself once wily, cunning selfish, worldly-minded; his name too truly was Jacob, "supplanter." But he became a converted man; as much so, and as truly so, as his degenerate descendant standing at the brink of his fountain. From being the supplanter, his name was changed into "Israel," "the soldier of God."

And what, in both cases, was the turning point in their spiritual histories? It was the sight of Christ; the revelation of His person and character and work. It was on a memorable night, (twenty years before the wrestling with the Angel at Jabbok,) on the stony pillow of Bethel, that Jacob received his earliest revelation of re-deeming love. The supplanter dreamed a dream. He saw a ladder planted between himself and heaven; or, as some think, his dreams took their shape and coloring from the physical features of his nightly solitude—that these strange, white, grey stones in the desolate moorland, formed themselves into a colossal staircase, leading up to heaven; at the base of which the outcast wanderer slept, angels beckoning him upwards, and the God of Abraham smiling upon him a welcome. It was a type of Him who was to be revealed as the way to the Father; "the way and the truth and the life," conducting the most foreign and outcast into the holiest of all. He rose refreshed and comforted: "This," He exclaimed, "is the gate of heaven! "And that first and earliest revelation was com-pleted and confirmed at the memorable night of soul-struggle, of which we have just spoken, where he wrestled, and prevailed, and saw the angel Jehovah face to face. What was revealed to him at first in type, was revealed to the Samaritan woman in visible real-ity and by living word. It was the manifestation of Christ in the glory of His person and fullness of His grace, which demolished in her case, too, the strongholds of Satan, and redeemed them for the service and glory of her accepted Savior!

And the same mighty power, the power of the cross, can van-quish and subdue us—can transform us who were once rebels, traitors, supplanters, into "soldiers of God." How many, touched by that omnipotent grace and by the attractions of that cross, are ready to utter the same glad and grateful testimony—

"See me! see me! once a rebel,
Vanquished at His cross I lie!
Cross—to tame earth's proudest able,
Who was e'er so proud as I?
He convinced me, He subdued me,
He chastised me, He renewed me;
The nails that nailed, the spear that slew Him,
Transfixed my heart and bound it to Him;
See me! see me! once a rebel,
Vanquished at His cross I lie!"

THE CONFERENCE
(continued)

When a Samaritan woman came to draw water, Jesus said to her, "Will you give Me a drink?" John 4:7

Each one of us must come, at some time or other, to have a personal dealing with Christ. It may be at one of those crisis-hours of existence, of which few are ignorant, when the even flow of life's current is arrested; when, to use the suggestive simile of this narrative, the pitcher is drained and emptied, and we are summoned away from our Shechem-homes and broken cisterns to seek supplies of some better 'living water.' It may be at a dying hour. It *must* be on the Great Day of Judgment. Blessed for us if that solemn and all-momentous conference and interview has already taken place—if we have already listened to His words of wondrous mercy—let down our vessel for the draught in the deep well of His love, and drank of that perennial stream which quenches and satisfies the soul's thirst forever!

The sinner who now confronted her unknown Savior at Jacob's well, as we shall afterwards find, was not—*could not,* with all her simulated lightness of soul, be happy. She had no part, and knew she had none, in the blessings of the true Gerizim. If she ever recalled, in her journeys to and from the fountain, Joshua's old rehearsal of promise and threatening, more than one curse must have thundered its anathema over her head; and although the many thousands of Israel were not there to respond, her own guilty conscience must have uttered its assenting 'Amen.' But as at that same memorable scene of patriarchal days, the Ark of the Testimony was placed between the adjacent hills, so now did the true Ark stand between her and the Ebal of curses, directing and conducting her up to the Mountain of blessing, and saying, "Woman, your sins are forgiven you." Shechem, her ordinary dwelling-place, was one of the old cities of Refuge. She may possibly have seen with her own eyes the manslayer hastening with fleet foot along the plain of Mokhna, up the narrow Valley she had just traversed, to be safe within the appointed walls from the avenger of blood. That Old Testament institution and type had, in the Adorable Person standing by her side, a nobler meaning, and fulfillment. Though all unconscious at the moment of her peril and danger, He was to her the great antitypical Refuge from the avenging sword of that law which she had so flagrantly outraged in heart and life.

"Jesus said to her," briefly, abruptly, "Will you give me a drink?" That request is preferred in the first instance for Himself—uttered as an introduction to the subsequent converse. But it is evident He wishes to put it in another and far more urgent form into *her* lips as well as into ours. It is the call of unfulfilled humanity, in its unquenched longings after something more than perishable fountains can yield; a cry to which the world gives its ten thousand and mocking answers, all, however, telling of a thirst which, with anything short of the true answer, cannot be met or assuaged. It is the cry of the spiritually wounded or dying soldier on earth's battlefield in the rage of his moral fever—Water! water! water! "Give me a drink."

Thus does the Savior start the question. It is the keynote of the subsequent divine music. It regulates the strain throughout. It touches the chords of that tuneless soul, and waked up its latent slumbering harmonies. The long-sealed and hardened lips come to sing, (and the strange Music impels hundreds of her fellow-townsmen to sing, too). "Will you give me a drink:" "As the deer pants after the water brooks, so pants my soul after you, O God! My soul thirsts for God, for the living God."

We may, in the present chapter, regard the interview unfolded to us in the narrative, as exhibiting several features which *characterize those spiritual conferences to which we have just referred as still taking place at this hour between the Savior and the sinner.*

Christ often comes and speaks UNEXPECTEDLY. When that woman of Sychar left her home, never did she dream of such an interview. No thought had she but of going to replenish her empty pitcher. If she had been a modern Romanist, she might, on reaching the "holy well," have perhaps counted her beads and muttered her 'our Father', but only to return light-hearted as she went. All unlooked for was the advent of that Divine Stranger. Still more unexpected the mysterious conversation which resulted in the change of heart and change of life.

Is it not so still? How often Jesus comes to the soul unexpectedly. *Sickness* has with appalling suddenness struck that strong man down. It was but yesterday when he was at his desk, or pacing the exchange, or studying his ledger, in the ardent pursuit of gain and engrossing earthliness—strong in pulse and brawny in arm, no premonition of an arrest on all worldly schemings. By sudden accident, or fever, or disease, he is chained to a couch of pain and languishing; it may be a bed of death. For the first time the dreadful realities of eternity are projected on his sick pillow. He has been summoned in the twinkling of an eye from the Shechem of his earthly pursuits, secluded from the hum of busy life, 'the loud stunning tide of human care, and crime,' the excitement of secular interests, the scramble of money-making, and he is lying by the Bethesda pool of affliction, with the hot, fevered sun as of midday beating on his brow. He is for the first time conscious—unexpectedly conscious—of a Personal Presence there. "JESUS sat thus on the well, and it was about the sixth hour." A few days before, he had not so much as a thought about Christ or his soul, with its everlasting interests. If you had spoken of these, he would have resented the allusion as a mistimed and impertinent interference. But it is, in his case, as in that of the mounted persecutor of old on his way to Damascus, of whom we read, "*Suddenly* there shined round about him a light from heaven above the brightness of the sun; and he fell to the earth, and heard a voice saying to him, Saul, Saul, why are you persecuting me?"

Take another case. It is that of a household who have until now enjoyed a happy immunity from outer *trial*, who have been strangers to those shadows of death which have darkened the homes of others. Theirs until now has been a Shechem Valley, musical with streams and song of birds, carpeted with flowers and fragrant with perfumes. But clouds have suddenly gathered; the streams have been arrested in their courses; the birds have ceased to sing; the blossoms have drooped and withered "Man goes to his long home, and the mourners go about the streets." At times, too, (not infrequently,) these are households where the Divine Redeemer has until now been a stranger, His name not hallowed, His love not felt, His presence not realized. But now He comes unexpectedly, as He did that night on Gennesaret, saying amid the wailings of the tempest, "It is I!" or, in the beautiful imagery of the Apocalypse, when the long-rejected voice is suddenly heard—its tones no longer disregarded—"Behold, I stand at the door and knock." Some loved one has been borne away to *the narrow house appointed for all living*, leaving in swept and desolate homes and hearts the irreparable blank: but in that hour of inconsolable earthly sorrow, the Divine Wayfarer of Sychar, now *the exalted Sympathizer on the throne*, draws near, and says, in tones of ineffable love, 'Sorrowing one! I will come in the place of your loved and lost. Your golden goblet is emptied; your earthly pitcher is lying in fragments about the well's mouth. But trust Me. **I** have broken these perishable cisterns, to lead you to imperishable ones. I will be to you more and better than all you have forfeited. I am the True Well of living water springing up into everlasting life.'

Or, to take yet another illustration. That worshiper came to the House of God, if not to scoff, at all events careless and uninterested in the stale message of the preacher—a reluctant victim and martyr to the conventionalisms of the age. No tongue had he to sing; no heart to pray, no desire to listen. Let the tedious moments be dragged out, the tiresome penance completed, and the congenial world, as soon as may be, return again. Ah, but a certain one, surer and more unerring than the Syrian archer on the heights of Ramoth-Gilead, drew a bow at a venture. The arrow sped forth with its message of death and life. Again the Damascus midday scene is repeated. Suddenly "the shining light which unhorsed the persecutor brings yet another Saul to the earth; and as suddenly and unexpectedly as in that solemn moment a voice speaks: "And the Lord said, I am Jesus whom you are persecuting: it is hard for you to kick against the goads." This worshiper left his home, like the woman of Samaria, with nothing in his thoughts but the earthly pitcher and the perishable streams. He leaves the sanctuary—he leaves the wayside-well, with this new song in his lips—

"My heart is fixed, eternal God,
Fixed on Thee;
And my eternal choice is made:
Christ for me!"

Christ often comes and speaks to the sinner when he is alone. The woman of Samaria was alone when Jesus met her. Had it not been so—had she been in company with others from the city—had she come at evening hour, when the wells of Palestine are alive with herds and flocks and drawers of water—it would have rendered close and prolonged conversation impossible. But with no other eye or ear to disturb or distract, her deep-rooted prejudices would be calmly combated, her sin detected and denounced by the unerring Censor at her side, and the light of heaven admitted to her darkened soul.

It is when alone—in the solitude of the sick chamber, or in those solitudes of life already spoken of, created by bereavement and death, that Christ comes nearest to the soul, and speaks at once most solemnly and most comfortably home to it. *The great questions of salvation and eternity cannot be weighed and pondered in a crowd.* The ruts of busy life jostle them in confusion. The whirl of business, the frivolities of society, the oblivion-power of the world, come with their tidal wave and sweep the impressions away. Another convicted sinner of the Gospels—we trust, too, another stricken penitent—is the picture and type of many a sinner still. "Jesus was left *alone,* and the woman standing in the midst. When Jesus straightened up, and saw *no one but the woman,* he said to her, . . . Neither do I condemn you: go, and sin no more." (John 8:9, 10.)

Even in regard to His own people, the Savior loves to speak to them alone; when, separated from the absorbing power of outer things, (it may be even Christian activities for the time suspended,) they obey the call He Himself of old addressed to His disciples, "Come apart into a desert place and rest a while." The ordinary occasion for such seasons of lonely silent conference is unquestionably the closet. The 'still hour' is the hour of prayer. Not even will the public services of the Sanctuary make up for this. These latter are the times for the jubilant multitudes crowding around the golden goblets of water brought up on the great day of the feast, amid hosannahs of joy, from the pool of Siloam.

But this is the meditative silence and seclusion by the well of the Patriarch, when the soul is alone with its divine Redeemer. It is the brook Jabbok we spoke of in previous chapters, where Jacob was "left ALONE," and there wrestled a man with him until the breaking of the day. Had he not been alone, there would—there could—have been no such wrestling, no new name, no spiritual victory; and as a Jabbok, so still, in the words of an old divine, "the battle of the soul is lost or won in the closet."

But it is not Christ's conversation with true *believers* to which we are now adverting, but rather to His first solemn conference with the *sinner.* It is often in times of loneliness and solitude that He speaks to him *most loudly, most solemnly, most tenderly.* How many may be able to tell of such seasons? Reader, do you not vividly call to remembrance that hour, when the very Gerizim of your worldly blessings, with its usual sunshine, was mantled in thick darkness; when, with sad heart and sorrowing step, you left the busy world behind you, and went forth, in the loneliness of your bereft spirit, (you knew not where,) in search of peace and comfort, which the once-smiling valley of life could not now give, for it had been changed into the Valley of the Shadow of Death? do you remember, when bowed to the dust in the presence of the King of Terrors, who had stamped mockery on your dearest earthly treasure, how amid the stillness and solitude of that darkened house and hushed chamber there was a new voice that for the first time broke the dreadful mysterious silence? You felt yourself alone with Jesus; and your experience was that of Job, who, not when his cattle were feeding around him in abundant pastures, his family unbroken, and his own health unscathed, but when all had passed away like a wild dream of the night, and he was left with nothing he could call his own but the bed of ashes and the broken potsherd—then, yes, then—in that hour of wondrous loneliness, these fevered leprous lips sang aloud, "I know that my Redeemer lives."

We repeat, the ear will not, *cannot,* give earnest heed amid the world's distractions and petty cares, and poor, flippant, superficial pleasures. Hagar of old would never have sought for the well had she not found herself in the midst of the *desert.* The soul would often never seek for Christ or find Him but for the solitary places of affliction. "Behold, "says the Lord, in a beautiful passage in Hosea, where He speaks of Israel in the midst of utter alienation and spiritual debasement, "I will allure her, and bring her into the *wilderness,* and will speak comfortably unto her," (lit. will speak to her *heart,)* "and I *will* give her her vineyards from there." In the very place where vineyards are least looked for, (the depths of the arid wilderness,) there, says God, speaking metaphorically, there, in the midst of the wilderness of trial, in these unbroken solitudes of the soul, where all green grass is burned up, no sheltering rock to screen from the flaming sun—where earthly shelters have perished, and earthly voices are hushed for the forever of time—that is the hour for my "speaking to the heart."

As it was when *alone* with the dead, the Prophet of Cherith raised up the widow's son, "so that the soul of the child came unto him again and he revived," so, often it is with Jesus in the case of the "dead in trespasses and sins." In the loneliest, dreariest spots of the Valley of tears, with barren mountains all around, amid the desolate sense of human isolation and friendlessness, the spirit catches up the sound of heavenly music—"It is the voice of my Beloved! Behold, He comes leaping upon the mountains, skipping upon the hills!"

Or, returning to the picture of John's narrative, how many, holding life's empty pitcher in their hand, bereft, companionless, having nothing in their unsolaced hour to draw with, for the well of their affliction is deep, have been admitted then and there into the heavenly household, and had, in their spiritual experience, the

Psalmist's beautiful words to the lonely fulfilled: "God sets the solitary in families; He brings out those who are bound with chains."

We observe yet once more, *Christ often speaks in the midst of the ordinary duties of life.* The woman of Samaria, while she was alone, was engaged, too, in the most commonplace occupation—drawing water at a Palestine well; and while doing so, Jesus meets her, and speaks to her of spiritual verities through the earthly element. He who called one apostle while at his ordinary occupation at the custom-house of Capernaum, and four others from their nets at Bethsaida—summons here another disciple when she had gone on the everyday errand of replenishing her pitcher for household purposes. He thus beautifully, though *indirectly* puts His seal on the sanctity of life's daily drudgery. He speaks to a Samaritan female, not only when employed in this her most ordinary duty, but He makes pitcher, and rope, and well—these common material things she was dealing with—the vehicles, so to speak, for imparting deathless spiritual truths to her soul.

There is a lesson to God's own people in this too. We have just adverted to the desirableness of occasional seasons of loneliness and seclusion, to afford opportunity for contemplation and prayer. But we must qualify this with the counterpart and complementary truth; the "not slothful in business" must dovetail with "fervent in spirit." Men are ever apt to rush to extremes. The *monkish* theory and practice is religious retirement and loneliness caricatured—loneliness in its exaggerated and abnormal form, in which life, real, true life and vigor, mental and spiritual, is rendered impracticable. In the case of the man of the world again, in the sensuous and irreligious sense of the term—the man so absorbed and engrossed with the pursuit of perishable gain on the one hand, or with sinful excitement and pleasure on the other, as to leave no room or thought for higher interests—here also the only true life of the soul, is overpowered, paralyzed, strangled. In spiritual things, as in most other, the *middle road* is the safe one; where the active and the contemplative are intermingled and blended; where worldly work is nobly, honestly engaged in, but not permitted to exercise an overmastering, absorbent power; where there are solemn hours and moments in which the valleys of busy life are left behind; when the pitcher is set down by the curb-stone of the well, and, with folded arms, and eyes intent on the Great Teacher, the mind forgets the household care, the noontide drudgery, and the material is merged in the spiritual.

Never allow the thought to disturb you, "Can this be lawful?

can this be Christian?—this constant wearing contact with dull, earthly pursuits—these poor little, lowly, petty anxieties, that are fretting away precious moments." If your complaint or confession is that yours is an idle, do-nothing life, we have nothing to say to that. There is more work for Satan in such case. But never fear healthy, invigorating, worldly occupation. God has sanctified it, because He has Himself ordained the sweat of the brow. And while He can meet His people at all times and under all circumstances, He loves to meet them in the pursuit of ordinary duties—yes, the lowliest and the humblest—with the pitcher on the head, or the draw-rope at the well, or the broom or shuttle in hand—Zebedee's children with their nets; David and Amos with their herds and flocks; Elisha with his plough share.

> "We need not bid, for cloistered cell,
> Our neighbor and our work farewell,
> Nor strive to wind ourselves too high
>
> For sinful man beneath the sky.
> "The trivial round, the common task,
> Would furnish all we ought to ask,
> Room to deny ourselves: a road
> To bring us, daily, nearer God."

We close, as we began, with the great question for us: Have *we* had our conference with the Savior of Sychar? It matters not whether He may have come to us suddenly and unexpectedly— when we were alone or in the crowd. But have we met by some of life's wayside wells; and whether prosperity or adversity were our portion—whether our pitchers have been full or empty—have we listened to His divine voice and closed with His great salvation? It was His first meeting with that Samaritan female; and never are the appeals and words of Christ so impressive as when He first speaks to the soul. If that woman had listened in vain—had she heard all His pleadings unmoved, and returned hardened and reprobate as she came—little would have been the likelihood of any subsequent impression under the same circumstances.

It was springtime around her in plain and valley; all nature was robed in its earliest green; the trees were putting forth their bud; the song of birds was welcoming the reviving earth. It was springtime in her soul. The storms of life's dreary winter had passed over her. She seemed, a moment before, a tree twice dead, plucked up by the roots. But the Sun of Righteousness was shining; as He shone, the sap, defiant in her case of nature's analogies, rushed up through the dried and wasted tissues, and the withered stem became clothed in summer glory! What if that day's convictions had been resisted, and the cumberer had despised the offered dews and heavenly radiance?

My brother, see that you do not refuse not Him who speaks. See that you resist not first convictions. If it is springtime too with your soul, let not the young bud be nipped, let not the young shoot be blighted, when it is putting forth its tender leaves. But listen to the divine Pleader as He thus calls you in the words of the Son—

"Lo! the winter is past,
The rain is over and gone,
The flowers appear on the earth,
The time of the singing of birds is come,
And the voice of the turtle-dove is heard in our land.
Arise, my love, my fair one, and come away."

RIVAL RACES

"The Samaritan woman said to him, 'You are a Jew and I am a Samaritan woman. How can You ask me for a drink? For (For Jews do not associate with Samaritans.)"—John 4:9

"Give me a drink," said Jesus, opening the conversation that was to issue in such momentous results.

An answer, probably such as He had anticipated, was returned, "You are a Jew and I am a Samaritan woman. How can You ask me for a drink?"

These words open to us an instructive, a painful chapter in human nature. The creed-feud—we had almost said the blood-feud—existing between Jew and Samaritan, has had, alas! its thousand lamentable illustrations and repetitions in the history of the world. Though involving a brief historical explanation, it will be necessary for the comprehension of the narrative that we advert to the cause of this fierce and fiery antagonism between the conterminous races—the dwellers in the same land, whose social and religious unity seems thus to have been so hopelessly destroyed.

The first Assyrian conquest of the kingdom of Samaria took place under Tiglath-Pileser. The wealth and nobility of the land of Ephraim were on that occasion carried forcibly away to Central Asia. A second and more sweeping invasion occurred under Shalmaneser; while the total depopulation of the country and the extirpation of the inhabitants, seems to have been consummated in the reign of this conqueror's grandson, Esarhaddon. He, however, in his turn repeopled the now desolate territories, not with restored exiles, but with a colony of aliens from the Tigris and Euphrates. During the interim, while the nice fertile lands were evacuated and left to waste and silence, the wild animals from Hermon and Lebanon, and the adjoining jungles of the Jordan, had taken possession of the dense and rank untended vegetation of the mountains and valleys of Samaria, and, as was natural, spread terror and dismay among the new settlers. The lion, now unknown in that region, was conspicuous among these. The colonists became haunted with superstitious fears. They were Gentiles—Pagans. But on this very account, being worshipers of 'lords many and gods many,' what was to hinder them adding one more deity to those they had imported from the East? By doing homage to the local god of the new country, they might propitiate his wrath, and have these wild beasts driven away, which, they doubted not, were the messengers and executioners of his vengeance. How were they, however, to attain a knowledge of the creed and rites of the old inhabitants, so as to graft and incorporate these on their own? They adopted the expedient of asking their distant conqueror to send from among the captives by the rivers of Babylon, one of the priests of Israel, who would indoctrinate them in the worship of the God of Jacob, or, as they expressed it, "teach them the manner of the God of the land." The request was complied with; and the result was the framing of a strange, enigmatical, compound worship—a hybrid between Judaism and Paganism. The captive priest took up his abode at Bethel and having imbibed the ecclesiastical laxity of Jeroboam's age, he had probably only too readily accommodated himself to the religious presuppositions of his new disciples, and taught them to worship the one spiritual Jehovah of Israel through some visible symbol—other imported idols adorning, or rather desecrating and defiling, the sacred place. The colonists from Media and Persia, or "Cutheans," as they were called, were subsequently supplemented by Greeks and Phoenicians at the time of the conquest of Alexander the Great. These, in their turn, brought a fresh accession of false gods to the paganized territory—Baal and Ashtaroth, Minerva and Jupiter—or, as this religious medley is described in the Bible narrative, "They feared the Lord and served their own gods."

The one only portion of the old Jewish creed which seemed to have been sacredly retained, (and which, after a lapse of thirty centuries, continues intact and inviolable to this day among the handful of representative modern Samaritans,) was the five Books of Moses. Rejecting all the other prophetical writings and later Jewish traditions, the Samaritan Pentateuch has remained to this hour a sacred heirloom in their synagogue at Shechem. In later years, indeed, they had evidently shared in some of the nobler beliefs of their neighbors—notably that specified by the woman of Samaria in the course of her conversation—an indefinite expectation of the coming of a Messiah. From all we have advanced, however, it is evident that the new kingdom was essentially composed of sensuous and sensual idolaters who had no inheritance in the blood of the ancient chosen people, and to whom pertained not the adoption or the covenants. They were a heathen colony planted in the very midst of Palestine, aliens from the commonwealth of Israel, and strangers to the covenants of promise. A few Hebrew women and slaves—possibly a few vinedressers and husbandmen—as we find in the case of the Jews at the time of the Babylonish captivity, were all that were left of the old inhabitants, so that their descendants could only by the slenderest links retain a claim to hereditary descent from the patriarchs of the land, Abraham and Jacob, Rachel and Joseph.

We have a remarkable proof, indeed, in the very words of our divine Lord Himself, how thoroughly Samaria was heathenized, and identified with Gentile territory. When He sent forth His seventy disciples, it could be, in His case, from no unworthy popular prejudice or antagonism of race that He gave this strict injunction, "Do not enter any towns of the Samaritans." The explanation is evident. His gospel was in the first instance to be proclaimed to the Jews alone, "to the lost sheep of the house of Israel;" and it would have alike contradicted prophecy, and marred and neutralized the exclusiveness of this primary offer, if the Gentile Samaritans, who had so little in common with the Jews, had shared in the benefits of that earliest apostolic mission. Such being their *heathen descent and half-heathen creed*, it is not difficult to understand how the old kingdom of Judah and Benjamin should, from the first, have entertained a rooted and unconquerable aversion to the aliens. Circumstances, year after year, tended to widen this separating gulf, aggravating and intensifying the mutual antipathy. On the return of the Jews from their captivity under Zerubbabel, these suspicious and untrustworthy Samaritans made offer of their friendship and good offices, to help the returned exiles in rebuilding their walls and temple. It was sternly refused. If the former had been the genuine representatives of the old ten tribes, the others might have overlooked past jealousies; and for the sake of the national unity have hailed them as auxiliaries. But not a stone of their sacred walls is to be touched by Assyrian and Greek colonists, who had so basely compromised and mutilated the religion of their fathers. Therefore, with reference to this very proposal to assist their southern neighbors, they are spoken of, not as "Samaritans," but under the unmistakable title of "the adversaries of Judah and Benjamin." The result showed, that patriotic far-seeing Ezra had not miscalculated their duplicity and treachery; for, stung to the quick by this rejection, they immediately set themselves by every means to impede the work of the rebuilding of the temple on Zion, and joined with the children of Edom in the cry, "Raze it, raze it, even to its foundation," (Ps. 137:7.)

This they could not effect; but, to carry out the spirit of revenge and rivalry, they determined to outdo the restored capital and temple of the south, by the erection of a still nobler temple on the top of their own Gerizim. In 420 B.C., this new and magnificent temple, arose. Alexander the Great, then with his army before Tyre, not only sanctioned its building, but sanctioned the appointment of an unprincipled Jew of priestly lineage (Manasseh) to be its first hierarch. The worship set up in this rival temple was the embodiment of all that strange jumble we have described, of heathen mythology and diluted and desecrated Judaism. It remained to crown the summit of their holy mountain for two hundred years, when it was destroyed by John Hyreanus, a Jew.

Meanwhile, however, the animosity of the northern and southern kingdoms if possible increased, as did also the moral laxity and debasement of the Cutheans. Shechem became the refuge of vagabond Jews: the unclean and excommunicated in Judah and Jerusalem—the libertines who rebelled against the needed reforms of Ezra and Nehemiah—found a ready asylum in Samaria.

Perhaps of all the religious battlefields this world has been compelled in sadness to witness, none has bequeathed such lamentable memories of exasperation and deadly hate: not even those disgraceful feuds (a scandal to Christendom) on the same sacred soil of Palestine, which the Mohammedan and Turkish soldiery at this hour gaze upon in dogged silence, as they see Greeks and Latins closing at times in mortal strife, on the occasion of their most sacred anniversary and at their most reputedly sacred place—the traditional Holy Sepulcher. The Samaritan sought, by every petty annoyance, to fret and irritate the Jew, and the Jew was not slow or reluctant to retaliate in kind and degree.

Samaria, as we have previously seen, was the nearest road for the caravans of northern pilgrims going to the feasts in Jerusalem. The Samaritans churlishly refused these the poorest rites of hospitality, and compelled them often to avoid maltreatment, by taking the circuitous and more fatiguing route by the Jordan Valley. Again, it was one of the few consolations enjoyed by the bands of exiled Jews in Babylon, to have announced to them, by means of the only ancient telegraphic communication—beacons on the mountain-tops—the appearance of the paschal moon. The first beacon-fire was lit on the summit of Olivet, and thence caught up from mountain to mountain in luminous succession, until, within sight of the Euphrates, they could, for the moment at least, take down their harps from the willows as they remembered Zion and its holy solemnities. But the Samaritans indulged the mischievous delight of perplexing and putting them out of reckoning by the use of false signals. Another wicked and successful exploit is recorded; and occurring as it did under the government of Coponius only a few years previous to the gospel era, may have tended at this time to deepen these animosities—A band of Samaritans succeeded in stealing to the courts of the Temple of Jerusalem during the Passover season, and defiling the sacred precincts by scattering them with dead men's bones; thus incapacitating the Jews that year from celebrating the great Feast of their nation.

Yet, combined with all this, there was, on the part of the Samaritan, the proudest assertion of hereditary right and ancestral glory. The Jew was but of yesterday, compared with the descendants of Jacob and Joseph, and Jerusalem was a modernized capital beside the old walls of time-honored Shechem, with its oaks and terebinths, under which the Father of the faithful pitched his tents. In the words of a graphic writer, Shechem was the city of Joshua and the Judges—Zion that of David and the Kings. Shechem was Moscow; Jerusalem was only St. Petersburg. The Jewish Pentateuch was the handiwork of a modern scribe, unworthy to be named in the same breath with that written by Abishua, the son of Phineas, the grandson of Aaron!

The Jew was in no way behind in his boastful assertions of prerogative and prescriptive right, as well as in the manifestation of malevolence. An extract from the apocryphal book of Ecclesiasticus describes the intensity of the feeling—"There be two manner of nations which my heart abhors, and the third is no nation: those who sit on the mountain of Samaria and those who dwell among the Philistines; and that foolish people that dwell in Shechem." The Jew would refuse to eat with them; to do so, was "as if he ate swine's flesh." He denounced the Samaritan as a base time-server, who would not hesitate to purchase immunity from pains and penalties by forswearing Jehovah and kissing the impious shrine of Baal or Jove. He regarded him as unclean as the evaded leper; to harbor him in his house would entail a heritage of judgments on his children. The name 'Samaritan' became a byword of reproach. He was publicly cursed in the synagogue—cursed in the name of Jehovah, by the writing on the two tables of the law, by the curse of the upper and lower house of judgment. He was pronounced unworthy of eternal life, excommunicated alike from the Church on earth and the Church in heaven. The bitterest word of scorn the Jew could hurl at the Infinitely Pure One was this, "You are a

Samaritan, and have a devil."

The yet untutored apostles shared the same exasperated feelings, when they asked their Lord to call down fire from heaven on some Samaritan village. All worthy of remembrance is His gentle yet sharp reproof, "You know not what spirit you are of." A new spirit of love, in which hereditary hate and malevolence were to have no place, was to be grafted on the hearts of men. And while, as corroborating all we have said, it is stated in our narrative, in a parenthetical clause, "The Jews have no dealings with the Samaritans," it is striking to observe, how in the very same breath the disciples seem to contradict the statement. For they evidently had such dealings—it being distinctly asserted that they had "gone to the city to buy bread," How can we reconcile this apparent contradiction, but on the surmise, that they had already been so far instructed and educated by their divine Master into a more conciliatory spirit; led, in these temporal interchanges, to take down the unnatural barriers of separation, preparing the way for a higher, purer, nobler fraternity, which was, in one sense, to have its birthplace that day at the well of Sychar?

For the same reason, our Lord's request for water from a Samaritan, and a Samaritan woman, must have sounded equally strange. The very strangeness perhaps, of the request, and the kind tones in which it was given, may have made the astonished listener all the more ready to give heed to the conversation that followed. There was nothing remarkable, indeed, (as we see in the case of Eleazar and Rebekah, Moses and Zipporah,) for a wayfarer asking a female to draw water to quench his thirst. But what was no breach of courtesy or etiquette in Mesopotamia or Midian, was a startling violation of national prejudice when Jew and Samaritan met at Jacob's well. How beautifully is the comprehensive charity and love of the Great Philanthropist, in breaking down all these unnatural and wicked antipathies, illustrated in His own graphic parable of the Good Samaritan! Jesus rejected and condemned, as much as did His Jewish brethren according to the flesh, the half-heathen creed of the Samaritans. We shall come, in the subsequent narrative, to find Him boldly stating so to this woman, *"You know not what you worship)."* But He would enunciate and proclaim at the same time that great truth, which, alas! is so often ignored by all modern Churches—Greek, Roman Catholic, Protestant—that while there are errors, grievous errors, which we must deeply deplore, and against which we must manfully protest and contend, there are ever, among the adherents of these different creeds, to be found beautiful exceptions in moral worth and in kindly deed—men who, despite of their doctrinal errors, have the loving spirit—whose creed is their character; or whose character, rather, rises above all creeds and doctrinal formulas, noble in heart and nobler in life, who may well put their orthodox neighbors to shame.

Such is His lesson in the great parable of the Good Samaritan. "A certain man" who "went down from Jerusalem," had fallen a prey to Jewish bandits, lying bleeding amid the rough stones which still line the old robber-haunt. The priest and the Levite (the impersonations of pure Judaism) strut past without a thought of aid; while a "certain Samaritan," a chance traveler, far from his own home and all the sympathies of home, dismounted his horse, bound up the sufferer's wounds, poured into them the oil and wine he had brought for his own use. (and which, as a Samaritan, he could not get easily replenished from Jewish vendors,) set him on his own donkey, brought him to the wayside inn, and shared the very contents of his scanty purse. It was at the peril of the man's life and limb. He might have been falsely branded as himself the robber and plunderer, accused of the old crime of wreaking vengeance against a helpless Jew, and letting him feel the severity of Samaritan hate. But undeterred by all such fears and false accusations, this despised outcast and alien, heretic and schismatic, whom priest and Levite would doubtless, as they passed, eye with malignant scorn, proved in time of need the real philanthropist, the brother man. With what withering sarcasm (if we can dare use in its mildest sense such a word in connection with the holy Jesus) did He turn round to the captious questioner with the query, "Which now of these three was neighbor to him who fell among the thieves?"

Thank God, the principles of *religious toleration* are now better understood among ourselves in this age; although the monstrous records of the Inquisition of the Middle Ages, as well as the deadly strifes between Greeks and Latins, Druses and Maronites, to this day, show *how deeply rooted these religious animosities are in the corrupted human heart*, and how much need we have, amid all our modern civilization and enlightenment, to moderate the fervor and intensity of party and sectarian feeling. If such were the feuds between Jew and Samaritan, where, on account of the compromise of vital religious truth, there were at least substantial grounds for quarrel and schism, how should those bearing the name of their tolerant Master blush at the antipathies and party shibboleths which have no such palliation: soldiers fighting nominally under the same banner, but who, instead of cheering their comrades in the fight, are rather frowning on them with hard looks, upbraiding them with hard words, and leveling at them the curse and the anathema! There is no denying it, that *one of the saddest triumphs of the Evil One is, and ever has been, this virulence of party strife, this tendency to party isolation, ecclesiastical exclusiveness.* Even the Apostles, as may be remembered, were slow to relax their old narrow prejudices. It required a special miracle to enable Peter to rise above the trammels of exclusive Judaism, to teach him the magnificent truth which his "beloved brother Paul" subsequently proclaimed, that "God has made of one blood all nations of men to dwell upon the face of the earth." Be the prejudices of His disciples, however, what they might, their Divine Master at least gave no sanction to the contracted spirit.

It is instructive to observe how specially these same Samaritans were included in His last legacy of love. In oblivion of all the past, He thus frames His parting apostolic commission—"You shall be witnesses to Me, both in Jerusalem and in all Judea, and in Samaria, and to the uttermost part of the earth." Oh, for a like spirit! not to anathematize, but to *Christianize;* not rendering evil for evil, or railing for railing, but contrariwise, blessing; trusting in no boastful hereditary claims, the pride of creed or sect or ritualism, saying, in arrogant superciliousness, "It is not fitting to take the children's bread and to cast it to the dogs;" but remembering that Paul's weighty words have a Christian, as well as a Jewish meaning and significance—that *holy lives are the true exponents of orthodox principles.* "He is not a Jew who is one outwardly, neither is that circumcision which is outward in the flesh; but he is a Jew who is one inwardly, and circumcision is that of the heart, in the spirit, and not in the letter, whose praise is not of men, but of God."

The case and words of the woman of Samaria tell us too plainly, how possible, how common it is, for one of scandalous and flagitious life to be a bold religious sectary, a zealous partisan; to speak glibly and haughtily on ecclesiastical differences about "Father Jacob" and "this mountain," and to wonder that there should be such a violation of religious etiquette that a High Church Jew should hold parley with a Low Church Samaritan. Lutheran may be ranged against Calvinist, Prelatist against Puritan, Predestinarian against Arminian, Baptist against Anabaptist, State Church against Dissenter. But tell us, among all, (collectively and individually) who is doing most honest, earnest work for Christ and humanity—who, amid the robber haunts of evil, are pouring most assiduously wine and oil into the wounds of this bleeding world? and the answer will not be hard to give: "Which now of these, then, is neighbor to him that fell among the thieves?" God speed the time, (yes, then, and not until then, will the Millennium dawn,) when Christendom, now mangled with a thousand wounds, will have these 'deadly wounds healed;' when Ephraim (that is, Samaria) shall not vex Judah, nor Judah vex Ephraim; when the holy word, "Brotherhood," mimicked and travestied in these modern days in a hundred base forms, will have its true and noblest meaning illustrated and vindicated, in loving hearts, in a united Church, in a converted world!

"Down the dark future, through long generations,
The echoing sounds grow fainter and then cease,
And like a bell, with solemn, sweet vibrations,
I hear once more the voice of Christ say, 'Peace!'

"Peace! and no longer from its brazen portals
The blast of dismal war-sounds shakes the skies,
But, beautiful as songs of the immortals,
The holy melodies of love arise."

THE GIFT OF GOD
AND THE LIVING WATER

Jesus answered her, "If you knew the gift of God and who it is that asks you for a drink, you would have asked Him and He would have given you living water." John 4:10

In the preceding chapter, we considered the astonishment expressed by the woman of Samaria at having her religious scruples so tampered with, as to be solicited by a member of the rival tribe for a draught of water from the well of Sychar. We saw to what painful excesses these neighboring kingdoms had pursued their jealousies, social and ecclesiastical; indulging in mutual anathema and excommunication, such as has seldom been equaled in the war of race, and the often fiercer war of opinion. To such extremes, indeed, was this repulsion carried, that it would doubtless form matter of wonder to this female, how He who now sought the boon, unless very different from others of His countrymen, should have no conscientious scruple in touching rope or pitcher that had been defiled by alien hands. While, on the other hand, we might have expected her to repudiate the thought of these being polluted and desecrated by the fingers or lips of a Jew.

His answer in the circumstances must have sounded startling. Instead of the retort and retaliation for which she was doubtless prepared, He arrests her attention, and at once softens and subdues any resentful feeling by the reply, "If you knew the gift of God and who it is that asks you for a drink, you would have asked Him and *He* would have given you living water," and *He* would not have refused you; *He* would not have been so ungracious as to reject the request given by a toil-worn traveler. Uninfluenced and unbiased by any such selfish and contracted feelings, "He would have given you;" and given you something better, nobler than that earthly element: "He would have given you living water."

Living water! The mysterious suggestive words could not fail to arrest her attention; and more arresting still, as it always is, **the magic power of kindness**. Who could this be, in Jewish attire, speaking in the Jewish dialect, yet in words strangely conciliatory? so different, probably, from other Judean pilgrims she may have met, time after time, at the same spot, with whom she was used to engage in virulent and fiery debate and banter, meeting and parting with expressions of mutual contempt and scornful hatred. "Living water"—The expression may have stimulated better, profounder thought. She was evidently not a stranger to religious truth. Apart altogether from her knowledge (derived from their revered Pentateuch) of Father Jacob, and the great theme of ecclesiastical dispute as to the worship on Gerizim and Zion, she expected "Messiah, who is called Christ," one greater than the greatest of the prophets, who was to "tell all things," and the blessings of whose kingdom she may have heard that these prophets had, again and again, described under the similitude of refreshing water.

Be this as it may, the Divine Speaker, in rising above her sectarian prejudices, seemed at once to secure her interest. With a divine sagacity, He seizes on what was most likely to rouse and sustain her attention and gain the great end in view, her everlasting salvation. He makes nature His text. He who, on other occasions, took the sower at Gennesaret, the bread at Bethsaida, the vine on Olivet, the golden goblet and its contents at Siloam, to discourse of Himself and spiritual truths, takes the water at their side to symbolize and illustrate the better "wells of salvation." No more is said about the quenching of His own thirst. He merges His own lower needs in the higher, deeper necessities of one who has never as yet risen above the material to the spiritual. "Living water!" How that image from that day forward must have been enshrined in her heart of hearts. It must have been to her like the never-to-be-forgotten look which the Savior cast upon Peter; or the "Do yo love Me?" on the shores of Tiberias or the pronouncing of her own name to Mary on the resurrection morn; or the "Peace be to you!" breathed on the gathered disciples. Yes, ever afterwards, when, as a new creature, she trod her native valley, the ear of faith must have caught in every murmuring brook divinest music, every stream that furrowed the mountain sides must have sang the song of redeeming love, or been like an angel whispering to her, and beckoning her nearer to her Savior-God!

But giving these words a general application, let us refer more particularly to the two salient points in this reply of Christ—the two hinges, so to speak, on which this golden gate turns: "THE GIFT OF GOD, and THE LIVING WATER."

First, THE GIFT OF GOD. There is nothing in this world which is not a gift of God. Every morsel of the bread which perishes, the sunlight which gladdens us, the atmospheric air which sustains us, the fuel garnered deep down in earth's storehouses to warm us, the succession of seasons, the living streams which fertilize our fields, the waving harvests which crown the year with their plenty, the thousand tints of loveliness and beauty in garden, and dell, and forest; far more, the blessings which rejoice and consecrate social life—the wellsprings of gladness in our domestic circles; these are severally and collectively "gifts of God." "Every good and perfect gift is from above."

But what are these to the gift here preeminently spoken of?—the Gift of gifts—a gift whose magnitude transcends all thought and illustration—the Son of the Highest to become of human virgin born—the lisping babe of Bethlehem's lowly cradle—the God of eternity condescending to be a pilgrim on life's highway, that He might open living streams for the lost and the perishing? "God so loved the world (and who can ever fathom or exhaust the meaning of that **so**?) that He gave His only begotten Son." God's "Gift"—it was unpurchasable by money, the unmerited benefaction of Heaven—free as the desert pool to the thirsty wayfarer, who has only to stoop and drink!

And this greatest and mightiest Gift, moreover, consecrates and sanctifies all minor ones. As the sun glorifies with his radiance the tamest landscape and transforms the barren rock into a pyramid of gold; so are all earthly and material blessings glorified and beautified and sublimated by the beams of the Sun of Righteousness. Christ gives a new and enhanced value to every subordinate gift. He has been well likened to the numeral which, put before the unmeaning ciphers, invests them with peerless and untold preciousness. The very outer world of nature wears a new aspect when seen through eyes spiritually enlightened: all earthly discipline has a new meaning and when the minor gifts are blighted or diminished or withdrawn, there is ever the imperishable Gift remaining beyond the reach of vicissitude or decay so that we can say, as the woman of Samaria doubtless could, in all time following this devout conversation, as she looked around the beautiful valley of her habitation, "Although the fig tree shall not blossom, neither shall fruit be in the vines; the labor of the olive shall fail, and the fields shall yield no food; the flock shall be cut off from the fold, and there shall be no herd in the stalls: yet I will rejoice in the Lord, I will rejoice in the God of my salvation."

While feeling alive to God's goodness in His diverse other gifts, can we heartily join in the transcendent estimate of the apostle,

"Thanks be to God for His *unspeakable gift!*" Truly with this gift, having nothing "we possess all things." In Christ's glorified person as the God-man mediator "all fullness dwells." No earthly gifts can compensate for the lack of this. But the Gift of God can make up for the absence of every lesser earthly mercy. "All my springs are in You!"

> "Oh bounteous Giver of all good;
> Who are, of all Your gifts Yourself the crown,
> Give what You can, without You we are poor
> And with You rich, take what You will away."

The second main topic of the Savior's reply in this beautiful verse, is THE LIVING WATER. As by the expression "the Gift of God," He points to *Himself*, to His glorious Person and character and work—so, by "living water" He would seem to designate *all purchased blessings of His salvation,* beginning with pardon and acceptance here, and culminating in eternal glory and bliss hereafter. The twofold symbol or similitude seems to accord with a striking kindred figure in the closing chapter of Revelation, where this Gift of God, the glorified Mediator, is represented under His apocalyptic name of 'the Lamb,' as seated upon His throne; while proceeding from these sublime recesses there flows "living water," "the river of the water of life, clear as crystal." It is *the magnificent stream of gospel salvation to a dying world,* life and luxuriance and beauty up-springing wherever it wends its way. In other words, the expressive symbol of those priceless spiritual benefits which flow from the Person and meritorious work of the divine Redeemer—forgiveness, peace, adoption, sanctification, tranquility in life, victory in death, triumph in eternity.

And observe, it is *living* water. There is no glory in anything from which life has departed. The tiniest mountain stream that sings its living song on its way through moor and rock, has more true glory and beauty than the dark, inky, stagnant lake or pool. The tiniest flower or moss, or grass, have more true glory in them than the inanimate trunk of the giant tree lying prone on the ground. Why? Because the one is living and the other is dead. "A living dog is better than a dead lion." So is it with all dead lifeless things, wherein the soul has no part, and which are of the earth earthy, springing from the earth and returning to earth, the mere accidents of this fleeting existence, such as wealth, possessions, rank, worldly honors; in one word, mere material good and prosperity. You may call them streams, but they are not *living* streams. They dwindle and evaporate as they flow; they warble no music in the ear in the hour of waning nature; they are only summer brooks which are congealed in death's wintry, sunless valley. But these *blessings of salvation* are *living*, they touch the immortal part, they belong to the soul, they are deathless as the God who gives them.

And as the blessing of salvation (the water) is *living*, so also is the Fountainhead—He who is here called "the *Gift of God.*" "If you knew the Gift of God, and *who* it is (the Person) who says to you, Give me a drink; you would have asked of *Him*." It is not dead doctrine, dry formulated dogma which the soul needs, but a living Being. "My soul," says the psalmist, "thirsts for God, for the living God." Paul, in words often misquoted, and in the misquotation their sense and beauty mutilated and destroyed, thus exults, in what may be called a dying testimony, "I know," (not "in whom") but, "I know *whom* I have believed." It was not sects, or creeds, or doctrines, or churches, or ecclesiastical organizations, that the dying hero clung to, in the hour of departure, but the glorious *Person* of the divine Immanuel, the living Presence of the ever-living, ever-loving Savior—the Brother, the Friend on the throne, whom he had learned to love more dearly than all the world beside!

Two other thoughts still claim our consideration. We have incidentally likened this verse to a golden gate on two hinges. Expanding the figure, it may be added we have here **two keys** to open that gate.

First, There is the key of *FAITH*. How was the woman of Samaria to appropriate that "Gift of God" and that "living water," symbolizing the blessings of a priceless salvation? If she had apprehended at the moment, which she did not, all the meaning of this divine utterance, how many conflicting thoughts, we may well imagine, would rush to her soul, ready to overwhelm her in confusion and despair. What a barrier between her and mercy must be her life of flagrant guilt; lock upon lock, bolt upon bolt, must exclude her from all participation in these spiritual privileges. Truly, in her case she had nothing to draw with, and the well was deep—too deep for such a sinner as she! Or, if she can dare dream of pardon and peace, what a long process of preparatory reformation and self-mortification must be undergone; how often must she climb the heights of Gerizim to load its altars with penitential offerings and costly expiatory sacrifices. It must be through long months of tears and penances before she can weave the rope of creature-merit to reach the living water!

What says that Divine Being standing before her, and who has made to her the glorious revelation she as yet so dimly comprehends? *Belief* in His word, in His ability, in His willingness, is all that is required. "If *you knew* the gift of God, and who it is that says to you, Give me a drink, you would have asked and He would have given you." It was in figurative language what Paul translated into plain words in an analogous case of conversion, "*Believe* in the Lord Jesus Christ, and you shall be saved." Yes, Faith can remove mountains—mountains of sin! *Faith is a key which can fit the wards of every lock, the intricacies of every heart.* Faith brings the soul into immediate contact with the Savior. It reveals salvation as a glorious free gift, without works, or preparations, or merits, or penances; no rope to weave, no "golden goblet or jeweled cup" to fashion, before the living water can be brought to quench the soul's thirst.

As the beggar kneels by the running stream at the wayside, and bears the refreshing draught—the free gift of bounteous nature to his lips on the rough palm of his hands—so the vilest spiritual beggar in the rags of sin—nothing to draw with, the well of his own sins deep—can partake, without money and without price, of a free, full, everlasting redemption—"the gift of God which is eternal life through Jesus Christ our Lord."

Like 'Christian', immediately on reaching, with the outstretched hand of faith, the cross on the top of the hill, the load of sin rolls down to the bottom. Oh for faith, simple faith, to credit the divine testimony and accept the free invitation. If not at this stage in the narrative, the woman of Samaria could, doubtless at least subsequently, and that too until her dying day, thus sing of the "living water" and the "Gift of God," in the Spirit of the Simple words of Cowper—

"E'er since by faith I saw the stream,
Your flowing wounds supply;
Redeeming love has been my theme,
And shall be until I die."

And as *Faith is* one key here spoken of, so *PRAYER* is another. "You would have *asked,* and He would have given you."

How many blessings are forfeited by failing to use this key? How many are doomed to a life of spiritual poverty and starvation, for this reason, "You have not, because you ask not." While, on the other hand, how often is the divine saying verified and fulfilled, "I have not said to the seed of Jacob, Seek my face in vain."

We have, in another scripture example, a beautiful illustration of the combined power of these two instrumental means—faith and prayer. *Blind Bartimeus*, despite of his sealed, rayless eyeballs— despite of the thronging crowd that would intervene between him and the Great Physician, and drown his suppliant cry for help, *knew* the Gif of God: "When he heard that it was Jesus of Naza- reth, he began to cry out and say, Jesus, son of David, have mercy upon me." *See how faith and prayer together arrest the ear and the footsteps of Christ!* See how, together, they bring the blind soul, like this blind wayfarer, near to the Savior! In the sublime simplic- ity of the narrative, "Jesus *stood still.*" "And he, casting aside his garment, rose and came to Jesus. And Jesus answered and said to him, What do you want Me to do for you? The blind man said to Him, Lord, that I might receive my sight. And Jesus said to him, Go your way, your faith has made you whole," (Mark 10:46-52.)

Faith and Prayer! Would that we may know, experimentally, this blessed composite—the *two golden keys of the two-leaved gate of salvation!* To use the homely figure suggested by Sychar's well, *Faith is the rope* and *Prayer is the bucket* let down for the living wa- ter. The two are joined in the briefest and simplest of creeds and confessions—"Lord," (that is *prayer*)—"I believe," (that is *faith*)— "Lord, I believe;" and deep conscious unworthiness adds the sup- plementary petition, "Help my unbelief!"

Have *we* known, do we know, the Gift of God? or, sad alternative, are we among the number of those of whom it shall be said, "They *knew* not, the time of visitation;" over whom a despised Savior will utter the wail of rejected mercy, unrequited love, "If you, even you, had *known* in this your day?" "This your day." Blind Bartimeus, and the woman of Samaria, had, each in their different experi- ences, probably but that *one* day, the one chance of a Savior pass- ing by; in the case of the former, to have the eyes unsealed, and in the latter to have the deeper blindness of the soul removed. That one opportunity, foregone and forfeited, might never have been renewed.

Doubtless, with respect to this female of Sychar, the Savior saw how all-important was her immediate acceptance of the gift of salvation. As the omniscient Shepherd, He discerned her infinite danger—how this erring sheep was plunging deeper and deeper amid the wilds of an ever sadder ruin—how a few more days or months of wandering, among these bleak mountains of sin would have made her irrevocably and irrecoverably, "the sheep which was lost." But He has followed after her "until He finds her." He pleads with her—reasons with her—tells her of her dreadful danger and peril, amid these savage deserts of her wandering, and of the peaceful pastures and living waters she was guiltily disowning. In the beautiful but expressive imagery of the Song of Songs, thus does the Heavenly Bridegroom address her—"Come with me from Lebanon, my spouse, with me from Lebanon; look from the top of Amana, from the top of Shenir and Hermon, from the lions' dens, from the mountains of the leopards."

And what is her experience, as, obeying His summons, these perilous mountain heights are left forever? She is enabled to exult in *the Gift of God,* under the very image of these verses—"A fountain of gardens, a well of *living waters,* and streams from Lebanon," (Sol. Song, 4:8, 15.)

And the same grace that was free to her is free to us; the same living water offered to her is offered to us. The gospel is replete with invitations to the Fountain of life. The vision of Jacob's Well mingles with the closing utterances of inspiration: the last accents which "He who sat on the throne" bequeathed to the Church, when the vision and the prophecy were on the point of being sealed up, were these: "Let him who is *thirsty* come, and whoever will, let him take of the water of life freely." We are empowered and warranted to echo, in His name, the words of the Great Inviter—no barrier, no condition, no qualification is there in approaching that living stream:

"Just as you are, without one trace
Of love, or joy, or inward grace,
Or fitness for the heavenly place,
O guilty sinner, come.

Come, here bring your boding fears,
Your aching heart, your bursting tears,
'It is mercy's voice salutes your ears—
O trembling sinner, come.

Come, say 'the Spirit and the Bride;'
The stream is full, the channel wide;
Who wills may drink the living tide;
Your Savior bids you come!

THE WELL IS DEEP

"Sir," the woman said, "you have nothing to draw with and **the well is deep**. Where can you get this living water? Are you greater than our father Jacob, who gave us the well and drank from it himself, as did also his sons and his flocks and herds?" John 4:11-12

This is the reply given by the woman of Sychar to the address of the Savior. It is an answer which begins, at all events, deferentially. Her previous reply was that of a churlish, uncourteous Samaritan, startled and offended at the familiarity of a hated Jew: "How is it that you, *a Jew?*" But now the kindness alike in the tone and substance of His language has apparently disarmed the virulence at least of her dislike and antipathy, taken the rough edge off her sectarian prejudice, and she addresses Him with the respectful title of "Sir," or "Lord." The promise, however, in the opening of her reply is not sustained. She gradually lapses into the old feeling and expression of disdain. He had designed to elevate her thoughts to everlasting verities—from the well at their feet to the water of life. But she has no spiritual discernment to raise her above the material; the *human* supersedes the *divine*; what was spoken figuratively is taken literally. His golden gate of salvation becomes, in her hands, iron and brass. So true is it that "the man without the Spirit does not accept the things that come from the Spirit of God, for they are foolishness to him, and he cannot understand them, because they are spiritually discerned."

With no higher thought, then, than a supposed reference to Jacob's Well, she starts difficulties in her rejoinder. There is, first, the lack of any mechanical provision (rope or pitcher) to fetch up the water, this, as we previously noted, not being the public well of the city—"Sir, you have nothing to draw with, and the well is deep." And, secondly, if it were some other well or fountain he referred to which contained this living water, she repudiated the tacit claim of superiority on the part of a modern Jew over the illustrious Father who gave the well, and "drank thereof himself, his children, and his cattle." There is evidently an implied antithesis in her expression, "gave us the well," to that of Christ's words in the previous verse, "the gift of God."

Could this novel gift He speaks of with such emphasis (living water), dare be compared with the patriarchal gift which had consecrated the whole valley, and around which clustered the most sacred memories of her tribe and nation? Indeed, though beginning with the courteous salutation of "Sir," she would seem, with the passionate fire of her race, to wax indignant at the slur expressed or implied on her great progenitor. After all, had this stranger only muffled his reproaches and deep-rooted antipathies under a feigned and counterfeited blandness, while there lurked underneath an unworthy reflection on Father Jacob? And yet, too, with an inquisitive nature, we note her eager curiosity to discover who this traveler was.

Question follows question. "From where have You?"—"Are You greater?" Who can this be, to dream of any other, any better fountain? The most prudent and sagacious of all the shepherd patriarchs had deemed this the best in the neighborhood. It had proved sufficient for the supplies of a vast encampment, to the cattle that browsed on the pastures around. Who is this apparently weary, exhausted wayfarer, who speaks so mysteriously of some superior well of "living water?"

The second part of her reply might appropriately furnish a motto or illustration for one of the boldest and most meaningless heresies of these our times. If not of *apostolical succession,* she was a bold and brave upholder and defender of *patriarchal succession.* "Our *Father* Jacob," says she, in words of suppressed indignation. That name was with her a *charm.* That well contained *holy* water, because historically identified with the ancestor of her race. She speaks as if, moreover, her Samaritan tribe had a monopoly of the grace and virtue descending from the veins of old Israel. Her words are not, "Father Jacob," but, "Our Father Jacob."

We have already treated in full, in a previous chapter, the history of that Samaritan nation which, in the person of this female, claimed the rare and exclusive prerogative and blessing of being Israel's children. As we then saw, they had neither part nor lot in this assumed inheritance. They were aliens—a mixed multitude from surrounding heathen countries, strangers in birth and blood, and more alien still in creed and practice. The Patriarch would have repudiated and disowned the illegitimate offspring. His mantle had fallen on no such degenerate seed. The claim was spurious, absurd, presumptuous. She spoke of Jacob as *her Father,* when alike, she herself personally and her tribe collectively, had failed to inherit *the only true patriarchal succession, the legacy of his virtues and spirit.* She had not heard words, uttered by bold brave lips, not far from the place where she was at that moment standing, "Do not begin to say within yourselves, We have Abraham as our father: for I say unto you, that God is able of these stones to raise up children unto Abraham."

And what is the pretension advanced by the Sacramentarian body among the Romanists, and by a segment in a Church which otherwise we delight to honor as a great witness of God's truth, but which, were it represented by that section, would utterly forfeit and belie the name Protestant: what is the figment of 'apostolic succession,' but just the question of this Sacramentarian at Sychar—the clinging to some supposed mythical virtue descending from the Fathers and apostles of the Christian era—saying, as they address other Churches beyond their pale, "Are you greater than our Father Jacob who gave us the well?" "Our father Jacob "is their self-constituted claim—"us," to whom the well was given.

Of all heresies this is alike the most *preposterous* and the most *arrogant*. What are the grounds on which those speak with such boldness and exclusiveness—unchurching and unchristianising all others, whatever be their unmistakable symptoms of a deeper and truer life? What is this boasted charm of apostolic descent? or, in other words, who is this Samaritan tribe, with its succession of golden links descending through the centuries after the age of Constantine—links which impart an assumed validity to their own ordination alone, while invalidating and negativing that of all others? The ecclesiastics of the middle ages have about the same claim to the name and spirit and grace of the apostolic fathers, as the profligate and heathenized Samaritans had an exclusive claim to the name and spirit and Well of Jacob. It passes comprehension to an unbiased mind, to a plain reader of his Bible, to a plain reader of the facts of history—to a plain student of the simple stern logic of common sense, how any *monopoly of virtue* can be claimed through a *succession*, not of piety and purity and a noble heritage of Christian and primitive graces, but through a *succession of apostate bishops and debased popes*, many of whose private lives were so stained with every vice and crime, that to speak of them as inheriting, in any true sense, the patrimony of the apostles, were enough to stir the bones of these holy founders of the faith, like those of Elisha, to rise and mutiny at such an abuse and perversion of sacred language and sacred thought.

No! our Father Jacob gave 'the well' with no such prescriptive rights. No Samaritan body is entitled to extrude and ostracize Churches who, in simple faith and earnest zeal, are doing Christ's work, or claim any such monopoly of that name or that free grace which belongs to Christendom—which belongs to the wide world.

There is a clause in these verses which, separated from its original connection, may be made to suggest one or two profitable reflections with which we shall occupy the remainder of this chapter. "Sir, you have nothing to draw with, and **the well is deep.**" These words may be affirmed with regard to the insufficiency of *Reason*, apart from Revelation, in fathoming the deep things of God. Deep, unsearchable, inscrutable are the divine counsels. The name of Jehovah, as the covenant angel said to Manoah of old, is "secret" or "wonderful." All the vastest problems which concern the human spirit and its relationship to God, and more especially the relationship of the sinful, conscience-stricken soul to a Being of infinite holiness and justice and truth, are *insolvable by reason.* Reason stands baffled at the well's mouth, exclaiming, "Oh, the depth!"

The world, for four thousand years, deifying Reason, strove to work out the solution. Greece, in the culture of her refinement and the wisdom of her philosophy, with all the possible data, which, apart from revelation, the human intellect could supply, addressed herself to this problem of the ages. But "the world by wisdom"— the mind of man in its highest condition of development and activity—"knew not God." All its shrewdest guesses were splendid but shadowy dreams, or rather gigantic failures. Human nature was a profound enigma. The high priests of her temple, professing themselves on these transcendental questions to be wise, became fools. There were on every side strange and puzzling aberrations, which Reason could neither explain nor reconcile—the harmony in the material world without—the disharmony in the moral world within—the glorious casing holding a broken, dislocated, tuneless instrument—the palace walls festooned and tapestried with all that is fair and lovely, enclosing a once royal, but now unsceptered and uncrowned inmate, with sackcloth on his loins, and the shadows of sin and sorrow on his brow. And more perplexing than all, how is that sackcloth to be taken off and the royal insignia refurbished and renewed? How are these tuneless strings to have the old harmonies restored? In one divine word, "How can man be just with God?"

Oh, proud baffled reason, "you have nothing to draw with, and the well is deep." The solution of the mystery of ages and generations is beyond you; as far beyond you as these distant planets are beyond the range of the naked eye, unassisted by the telescopic lens. But where *Reason* fails—where the well is too deep,

Revelation, like rope and pitcher, fulcrum and lever, comes to our aid. Yes, blessed be God; in this precious Bible, deep though the well be, we have the "something to draw with." Revelation speaks where reason is silent—unfolding to us the Divine method (undreamt of by human wisdom or human philosophy) for restoring the fallen—bringing the present discords of the inner world into harmony with the order and melody of the outer, and solving in the cross of Christ that mystery of mysteries, "How is God to deal with the guilty?"

The few brief words of the preceding sentence, uttered in the ears of this outcast wanderer of Samaria, had given a glorious response to a question on which all heathen and all reason's oracles had been dumb, "If you knew the gift of God, and who it is that says to you, Give me to drink, you would have asked of him, and he would have given you living water." Through that life and immortality which have been brought to light by the gospel, the little child, as well as the profound philosopher, can stand by that well's mouth and exclaim, "Oh, the depth!" But it is now with the apostle's addition, "Oh, the depth of the riches, both of the wisdom and knowledge of God!"

"Sir, you have nothing to draw with, and the well is deep." These words may be uttered with regard to the mystery of **God's providential dealings**. "The well is deep." Many a sorrowing broken-hearted one is brought to the well's mouth, and, stooping over the darkness, is heard to exclaim, "Your judgments are a great deep!" Here, in this imperfect world, there is nothing to draw with, nothing to gauge the "needs be" of the divine dispensations. The more we try, with our puny wisdom, to fathom the depths of Jehovah's dealings, the more unfathomable they are. The best, fondest, most treasured names are written on gravestones. Why is this? The vicious, the selfish, the false-hearted, the unthankful, the useless, are allowed often to live on, pampered with prosperity—the fabled horn of plenty pouring its contents into their lap; while the good, the kind, the true, the loving and beloved are either prematurely cut down, or go bowed with pain, or with penury, or with blighted affections to the grave—*This well is deep!*

The aged, the decrepit, the suffering, are often left to drag on an apparently useless existence. The old, gnarled, decayed trunks are spared, while the axe is laid at the root of the green sapling, the pride and beauty of the forest. Why is this?—*This well is deep!* The careless, indifferent herald of the truth—the unfaithful watchman of souls, is left to *slumber* at his post and *trifle* with his Master's work, while the bold standard-bearer in the battle of evil—the toiling, wakeful sentinel at home, the hero-heart in the mission-field abroad—have their weapons shattered in their hands, and the Church of God is left to exclaim, through her tears, over the irreparable blank, "My Father, my Father, the chariot of Israel and the horsemen thereof!"—*This well is deep!*

But why stand straining your eyes down the dark cavity? "You have nothing to draw with." Here in this imperfect state, *all is mystery.* All the earthly explanation of these deep, these 'great deep' judgments, is this, "Verily You are a God that hides Yourself." If you had rope and bucket, so as to descend the shaft and reach its unsounded depths, there would be no harsh verdict, no questioning the rectitude of the divine dispensations. Standing as you now are at the well's mouth, amid the glitter and glare of the world, you cannot understand or comprehend these *mysteries of life and death,* these *baffling enigmas in providence.* But the hour will arrive when you shall have the needed apparatus, when the profound secret of the divine works and ways will be revealed and unfolded. "In your light, O God, we shall see light." To use the language of Deborah's ancient song of triumph, there is at present 'the noise of archers' at the brink of the well. But the day is coming when we too shall be able to take up her joyous strain: "Those who are delivered from the noise of archers in the places of drawing water, there shall they rehearse the righteous acts of the Lord!"

There is a tradition regarding one of the other sacred wells of Palestine—the *Well of the Wise Men* between Jerusalem and Bethlehem—that when the Eastern Magi had at one time lost the guidance of the mystic star, while stooping over this fountain they saw it once more reflected in its waters; forthwith it guided them to the place where the young child was—"When they saw the star, they rejoiced with exceeding great joy." True, at all events, is this beautiful tradition regarding *God's providential dispensations.* At times we lose the guiding star; it is swept from our firmament; we travel on in darkness, in our unpiloted way—led in our sorrowful musing to exclaim, *"Where is now my God?"*

But when on our bended knees we stoop over the well—yes, often in our very darkest night of mystery and sadness—lo! the heavenly light reappears—we see the lost star of Providence mirrored in the fountain of salvation. *The work and the love of Christ explain what is otherwise often inexplicable.* God our Maker—God our Redeemer—gives "songs in the night."

"Sir, you have nothing to draw with, and the well is deep." These words may be affirmed with reference to the **veiling of the future.** Standing by the mouth of that well, looking down its unexplored cavity, "The well is deep." The future—that dark, ungauged, unfathomed future, how many a thought it costs! Yet it is a vain musing, a fruitless conjecture. "You have nothing to draw with." Even *tomorrow* has no pitcher that can be let down for a draught: you know not what a day may bring forth! The *past* we do know about, and there are special times when it comes before us with fresh vividness. Memory follows group on group, coming through the glades of the olive-forest to draw water; some with elastic step, and ringing laugh, and joyous song; some with mourning attire, and tearful eye, and broken pitcher; yes, some, unknown to themselves, to draw their last draught, to fill their last flagon: we lose them among the twilight shades; they are never again to return.

But from the standpoint of the present, who can forecast the doings at the well's mouth? who has rope or pitcher or plumbline to fathom the depth? Some may now be gazing, as the writer did from the literal Well of Jacob, on golden vistas, bars of glorious amber clouds stretched across the luminous horizon, lighting up with parting radiance Gerizim, the mountain of blessing; but before another week or month or year measures out its course, every such vista may be curtained with mist and thick darkness, Gerizim obscured from view, and *Ebal* alone, with its dark, gloomy grey, meeting their eye.

But it is well for us we cannot anticipate the future. Thank God for the gracious provision, "You know not what shall be on the morrow." Were the morrow unveiled, this world would be hung with curtains of sackcloth; there would be fewer happy hearts among us. *Inevitable trials*, of which, by a wise and kind arrangement of Providence we are kept in ignorance, would then project their long deep shadows athwart life's bright sunshine, and make existence itself one protracted period of anticipated sorrow. It is a merciful thing, when, ever and anon at solemn anniversaries, we attempt to cast a glance down the future, to hear Him who has that future in His hand saying, *"You have nothing to draw with, and the well is deep."*

Yes, but this is our comfort. Though too deep for *us*, it is not too deep for *Him*. He has the rope and pitcher in His hand; and whether, in drawing up the vessel from the unseen depths, it reaches safely the well's mouth, or is broken in the transit, all is appointed and ordained. "The Lord reigns." "Trust Me," He seems to say; "that Well is Mine. Trust me; that white, unwritten scroll of the future is Mine. It will be filled up by Me, whether in gleaming letters of gold, or with the dark lettering of sorrow." "Although you say you cannot see Him, yet judgment is before Him, therefore trust in Him."

THE CONTRAST

Jesus answered, "Everyone who drinks this water will be thirsty again, but whoever drinks the water I give him will never thirst. Indeed, the water I give him will become in him a spring of water welling up to eternal life." John 4:13-14

In the preceding chapter and context we found the thoughts of the woman of Samaria were of the earth—earthy. Nothing but the well at her feet presented itself to her dim unspiritualised vision, as the mysterious Stranger spoke to her of "the gift of God" and "the living water." Unrepelled by her *insensibility to divine realities*, the Heavenly Teacher pursues His theme; not, however, by answering her challenge—in vindicating the dignity of His own person compared with that of 'Father Jacob.' He had a higher end in view. He wished to raise, not only her, but all who in after ages would read this story of the wayside fountain, above the things of *earth* to "the river of God which is full of water."

Again, therefore, He recurs to His text, and continues the emblem by the announcement of a startling and significant contrast. He begins His reply with the assertion regarding the well of the Patriarch at which they stood, "Whoever drinks of this water shall **thirst again;**" an assertion which may appropriately be invested with a wider meaning, enshrining as it does the great truth, that *all creature and created-good is inadequate of itself to satisfy the yearnings of the human soul.* In every breast there is a craving after happiness. "Who will show us any good?" is the sigh, the soliloquy, of weary humanity. There are many streams of *created* enjoyment. Some of these lawful, innocent, exhilarating, which have the blessing and favor of God resting upon them. Others are poor, vile, degraded, unworthy.

But even the best and purest, viewed by themselves and apart from Infinite excellence, can afford no permanent bliss or satisfaction. They do not, cannot quench the immortal thirst. Pitcher after pitcher may be brought to the well's mouth; the golden goblet of *riches*, the jeweled flagon with the luscious draught of *earthly glory*, the brimming transparent pitcher drawn up by the silken cord of *human affection*. But He who knows the human heart pronounces, that "thirst again" is the property and characteristic of them all.

The finite can never be a satisfying portion for that which was born for the infinite. Satisfying portion! *Philosophy*, with its eagle soarings, says, "It is not in me." The pride of *rank*—crowns and coronets, and lordly titles—says, "It is not in me." The laurel of *conquest*, as it withers on the warrior's brow, says, "It is not in me." *Gold*, with its glittering heaps, laughs its votaries to scorn, and says, "It is not in me!" The most renowned of earthly conquerors seated himself by that well. He brought the monarchs of the world to be his drawers of water; each with his massive goblet going down for the draught, and laying the tribute at the victor's feet. But the tears of the proud recipient have passed into a proverb; and if we could ask him to translate these dumb tears into words, his reply would be, "Whoever drinks of this water shall thirst again."

But if such be the unsatisfactory nature of *earthly* happiness, the brokenness of *earthly* cisterns—what nobler compensations, what more enduring pleasures are there to take their place? You cannot attempt to dislodge one object of earthly affection or pursuit without having some other and better to substitute in its room. It was a dictum of the old philosophy that nature abhors a vacuum, and this is as true regarding the moral as the material world. The dove of old with weary wing, would have retained its unstable perch on the restless billow had it not known of an ark of safety. You cannot tempt the shivering child of poverty to desert his garret or crude covering, until you can promise him some kindlier and more substantial shelter. You cannot induce the prodigal to leave off the husks of his miserable desert exile, before you can tell him of a father's house and welcome. You cannot ask him to part with his despicable rags and tinsel ornaments until you can assure him of robe, and ring, and sandals. The husks and the tatters, wretched as they are, are better than *nothing*.

In one of the islands in our northern coasts, a daring adventurer scrambled down one of the steep cliffs which rose perpendicular from the ocean, in search of the eggs of some seafowl; the *precarious ledge* of rock on which he stood suddenly gave way, and with one giant bound plunged him into the boiling surge beneath. In a moment, the instinctive love of life made him spring from the yielding footing and lay hold on a branch of ivy which clung with uncertain tenacity to the precipice that rose sheer above him. Who would have had the madness or cruelty to shout to that wrestler for dear life, to let go the treacherous ivy branch? Worthless as it was, it was his only chance of safety; and those on the summit of the cliff, the spectators of his imminent peril, were wise, not by word or sign to disturb his grasp of what they anxiously felt might prove a brittle thread in these moments of suspense. But when a fleet foot had returned with the rope, and let it down by the side of the exhausted man, then, with no hesitating accents did they call upon him to *let go the fragile support* and lay hold of what brought him up safe to their feet.

In the same way do we find the inspired writers dealing with the human soul. They never are content with negative admonitions. They never exhort to 'abhor that which is evil,' without telling of some objective 'good' to which the heart can cleave in stead. "Charge those who are rich in the world that they do not be highminded nor trust in uncertain riches, BUT in the living God." "Love not the world, neither the things that are in the world... The world passes away, and the lust thereof; BUT he that does the will of God abides forever."

This is the procedure of the divine Redeemer with the woman of Samaria; conveying, through her and through the outer material symbol and similitude, a deeper moral lesson for 'all mankind.' He tells her, pointing to the well at her feet, that returning there day by day she would require continually to refill and replenish her emptied pitcher; but that He had nobler living streams in store which would quench her soul's thirst forever.

He says the same to us. As in her case, so also in ours, in a higher figurative meaning, *He does not condemn many of these worldly streams of innocent pleasure, or forbid their being resorted to.* The needs of the body, the claims of our physical and social natures are integrated with our moral and spiritual natures; for man is a complex being, with intimate relationships binding him to *both* worlds; and the imperious calls of the one, can as little as those of the other, be with impunity neglected or ignored. Jesus recognizes *both. He who knows our frame would lay no cruel arrest on many objects of lawful earthly pursuit—many wells of earthly happiness. All He says of them is, If you restrict your journeyings to these, you will not be satisfied—you will assuredly thirst again.*

But I have a well of living waters to tell you of, more far lasting than all earthly sources of supply. You will not require the glowworm and the starlight when you have the meridian sun; the shifting sand when you have the solid rock; the tiny stream when you have the infinite ocean. "Everyone who drinks this water will be thirsty again, but whoever drinks the water I give him will never thirst. Indeed, the water I give him will become in him a spring of water welling up to eternal life."

There are many salient points presented to us here. Space will only permit touching on one leading and beautiful thought suggested by the two central words of the latter verse; where all other *outer* objects of perishable pleasure are brought into contrast with that which is *inward*, "IN Him." "It shall be **in him** a well of water springing up into everlasting life." The believer has an inner well in his soul—something within the renewed being which makes him independent of all external earthly good and earthly happiness. Let *outer* things smile or frown, it matters not. That 'source of lasting joy' is no 'summer-dried fountain.' But being fed from the everlasting hills, it is always full, always flowing, overflowing.

What though the world grow false and treacherous? What though worldly means are abridged, worldly pleasures fade, or bereavements narrow the beloved family circle? The *inner* sources of truest peace cannot be invaded! Of the believer, outwardly impoverished, it can be said, as of the Church of Smyrna of old, "I know your poverty, but you are rich." In these *hidden sources of satisfaction and happiness* imperceptible to the eye of the world, we are furnished with a key and solution to *Paul's paradox*, "Having nothing, yet possessing all things." How often was the reality of this inward satisfying and sustaining good illustrated in the case of this great man? Look at the closing scenes of his life when a prisoner in bonds in the world's capital. See some of the pitchers which he brings up from this *inner fountain*, when all other shallow rills were rapidly drying in their channels. "Not that I was ever in need, for I have learned how to get along happily whether I have much or little. I know how to live on almost nothing or with everything. I have learned the secret of living in every situation, whether it is with a full stomach or empty, with plenty or little. For I can do everything with the help of Christ who gives me the strength I need. At the moment I have all I need—more than I need!"

Or see him in the same place, at a yet later period, when the earthly streams of comfort had well-near perished; lonely, deserted by man, he could yet, with the unimpaired energy of 'the life hidden with Christ,' write the glowing words, "All men forsook me. . . . Notwithstanding the Lord stood with me and strengthened me." Or again, when in the hour of sinking nature, his enemies were insulting his gray hairs, loading him with reproaches and indignities, and doing what they could to shake his constancy in his great Lord—when every other well and stream had deserted him—when his aged and tremulous arm could no longer fetch up the flagon from the failing earthly pool—when the pitcher was about to be "broken at the fountain," and the wheel "broken at the cistern"— the fountain of his soul's peace was clear and sparkling as ever. He seems to say, 'Attempt not to cloud my hopes or eclipse my faith. Dream not that I am to act the coward's part, and purchase immunity from suffering and death by base retraction. You may shut me off from all earthly streams of joy—you may bind heavier irons on these tottering limbs—you may threaten me with the horrors of the amphitheater—you may sprinkle my insulted ashes on the waters of your Tiber river, or scatter them on the wide sea, or by the winds of heaven; but "nevertheless I am not ashamed, for I know whom I have believed, and am persuaded that He is able to keep that which I have committed to Him against that day."'

If you asked him the secret and spring of all this superhuman faith and magnanimity and hope, he would reply in the brief words, "Christ *in me* the hope of glory." *Jesus*, in the glories of His person, and in the fullness and completeness of His work, was that inner fountain of gladness and peace, the "spring shut up, the fountain sealed"—and "when He gives quietness, who then can make trouble?" The apostle tells the Philippians what alone would prove the secret of their heart tranquility, as it was of his own, "The peace of God, which passes all understanding, shall keep your hearts and minds through Christ Jesus."

Is that peace *ours?* After, it may be, long vainly seeking peace—a resting-place for the soul elsewhere, have we returned to the true *Ark*—the refuge from the storm and the covert from the tempest? Has the true *Noah* put forth his hand and taken us in? and are we now, with folded wings, enjoying that, without which all outer calm is vain, illusory, worthless—reconciliation through the blood of the cross? "Therefore being justified by faith we have peace with God through the Lord Jesus Christ."

Reconciliation! Have you known the meaning of that word, even with regard to *earthly friends;* when, after years of bitter estrangement, the prodigal is locked in the arms of his father; or brother is reposed in the early love of brother; or sister is cuddled in the embrace of a long alienated sister?—what is this, compared to reconciliation with the Being of all beings, the Friend of all friends? For if God be for us, who can be against us? if God gives peace, who can give trouble? if God smiles upon us, who can really frown? If God be our reconciled covenant God and Father, then we have the sweet persuasion that all things are working together for our good; and even the very rills of creature bliss that were before in themselves unsatisfying, become invested with new elements of happiness and joy.

"I can truly say," to take the testimony of one, illustrious as a Christian, but illustrious too, among our country's scientific explorers, and who, escaping many treacherous reefs in the literal ocean, had reached the truer spiritual haven. "I can truly say, that I have found the ways of religion are ways of pleasantness, and all her paths are peace. I was never half so happy before I came to this knowledge, and never enjoyed so much of life. Pleasures or enjoyments which are sinful, have no temptations for me. But I have yet many rational enjoyments and pleasures—domestic pleasures, social pleasures, the pleasures afforded by communion with great and good men, and above all, the pleasure derived from a sense of the favor of God in the heart, which indeed passes all understanding. I used to fancy I must give up all enjoyments if I became religious. But now I find that things I used to call pleasures now disgust me, while a multitude of new enjoyments have burst upon me."

"How pleasant," says another beautiful and well-known exemplification of the Christian life, "How pleasant it is to have God for a friend, to know that He is about my path and with me. How pleasant it is to consider that nothing can hurt me, nothing can injure me, for God is my portion forever and ever. He feeds and will feed me; He supports and will support me. In Him I become independent of the world. I desire not riches, pleasures, or the favor of men. Having God I possess all things." "My days," says Doddridge, "begin, pass, and end in pleasure, and seem short because they are so delightful."

"I never knew happiness," said Wilberforce on his death-bed, "until I found Christ as a Savior." Oh, what a lever true religion is thus found to be in elevating the soul to the enjoyment of satisfying bliss! And how is it so? We answer again, because nothing *finite* can satisfy that which was made for the *infinite*. You might give to the eagle, of which we have spoken, a golden cage, and feed him by princes' hands; but this would never be to him an equivalent for his native, free-born, sun-ward soarings.

Water never rises above its own level; and so, the best of earthly joys and rills of pleasure can rise no higher than earth. They begin and terminate here. But the living water with which Christ fills the soul, springing from heaven conducts to heaven again. Flowing from the Infinite—flowing from the throne of God and of the Lamb, from the city of the crystal sea, it elevates to the Infinite! It finds its level in the river of the water of life which flows in the midst of the celestial Paradise. And just as on earth, so long as our mighty lake-reservoirs are full of water and the channel unimpeded, the marble fountain in street or garden, sends up, on the gravitation principle, its crystal jets in unfailing constancy—so (with reverence we say it) never shall these fountains of peace and joy and reconciliation and hope cease in the heart of the believer until the mighty reservoirs of Deity are exhausted; in other words, until God Himself ceases to be God. Everlasting life is their source, and everlasting life is their magnificent duration!

We have witnessed the memorable and interesting spot at the roots of Mount Hermon, familiarly known as 'the sources of the Jordan.' There, the river of Palestine is seen bubbling out of a dark cave, and thence hastens on through its long tortuous course to lose its waters in the *Sea of Death* (the Dead Sea). That is the picture and illustration of every stream of earthly happiness. They terminate with the grave. But this inner fountain in the hidden man of the believer's heart flows onwards to the *Sea of Life*; and the hour which terminates the worldling's happiness only truly begins his!

On the other hand; how awful the state of the soul continuing in guilty neglect of this 'living water.' Every well resorted to but the true well; partaking of all waters but the living waters; a stranger to the only satisfying good, feeding on *husks*, and starving for lack of the bread of life. You have heard of the rage of bodily hunger—what those may be impelled to in the agony of famine—in the straits of siege or shipwreck. You have heard how the very mother has been untrue to her deepest, tenderest instincts; or how the famishing crew on the wild untenanted shore have had to cast lots for nature's direst extremity.

But who can tell *the famine of the soul?* Alas! we cannot tell it, for we cannot now feel it. There are expedients to which we can, and do betake ourselves to stop that infinite rage of spiritual hunger. We throw *sops* to the immortal appetite. There are husks with which we can keep it down, messes of pottage to decoy from the true heavenly birthright. But when the husks are ended, what then? When life is ended, what then? When cast on the inhospitable shores of a bleak and ruined eternity, what then? It will be an unresponded-to cry, ringing its undying echoes, "I perish with hunger!"

You have heard of *the rage of bodily thirst.* Here is a picture of it from a graphic pen: "Many years ago, when the Egyptian troops first conquered Nubia, a regiment was destroyed by thirst in crossing this desert. The men, being upon a limited supply of water, suffered from extreme thirst, and deceived by the appearance of a mirage that exactly resembled a beautiful lake, they insisted on being taken to its banks by the Arab guide. It was in vain that the guide assured them that the lake was unreal, and he refused to lose the precious time by wandering from his course. Words led to blows, and he was killed by the soldiers whose lives depended on his guidance. The whole regiment turned from the track and rushed towards the welcome waters. Thirsty and faint over the burning sands they hurried, heavier and heavier their footsteps became, hotter and hotter their breath, as deeper they pushed into the desert, farther and farther from the lost track where the pilot lay in his blood; and still the mocking spirits of the desert, the phantom of the mirage led them on, and the lake glistening in the sunshine tempted them to bathe in its cool waters, close to their eyes, but never at their lips. At length the delusion vanished, *the fatal lake had turned to burning sand.* Raging thirst and horrible despair! the pathless desert and the murdered guide! lost! lost! all lost! Not a man ever left the desert, but they were subsequently discovered parched and withered corpses by the Arabs sent on the search."

Such is life—a mocking mirage, the phantom of the wilderness! Thousands, lured by the brilliant specter, hurry on in the chase after happiness, in hot pursuit after the vain and unreal. But all is illusive, ending in mockery and disappointment, 'as a *dream* when one awakens,' leaving the thirst of the deathless soul unquenched; and, unless a nobler Fountain be resorted to, this remains the irreparable doom, the unchanging destiny—"Him that is thirsty, let him be thirsty still."

But, thanks be to God, there is no such malediction now ringing in our ears. We may listen rather to one of the blissful cadences of the Bible—a sweet strain, a sublime harmony, wafted from the heights of heaven, "They shall HUNGER no more, neither THIRST anymore." It is further added, in the same beautiful passage, "The Lamb that is in the midst of the throne shall feed them, and lead them to LIVING fountains of waters." Yes, He it is, this slain Lamb of the Heavenly Paradise, who has solved the problem of human happiness. He is the true "Fullness," the *only satisfying Good*, groped after by the Platonic philosophy. "In Him all fullness dwells."

It is over the portico of the Gospel Temple, not over any heathen shrine, the superscription is written, "They shall be abundantly satisfied with the abundance of Your house, and You shall make them to drink of the rivers of pleasures!" What is to be our choice? The *phantom* or the *reality?*—the substance or the shadow?—the earthly waters, with their inseparable characteristic, "thirst again"—or the 'rivers of pleasures' springing up into everlasting life? At any moment the curtain of the seen and temporal may be rent in twain, and the world and all its hopes scattered like the leaves of autumn. As we are seated in thought at Jacob's Well, listening, from holy lips, to the contrast of the earthly with the perennial stream, may it be ours to breathe the fervent prayer:

"Hear me! to You my soul in suppliance turns
Like the lorn pilgrim on the sands accursed.
For life's sweet waters, God, my spirit yearns;
Give me to drink; I perish here with thirst!"

FIRST EVASION AND REPLY

The woman said to him, "Sir, give me this water so that I won't get thirsty and have to keep coming here to draw water."

He told her, "Go, call your husband and come back."

"I have no husband," she replied.

Jesus said to her, "You are right when you say you have no husband. The fact is, you have had five husbands, and the man you now have is not your husband. What you have just said is quite true."

"Sir," the woman said, "I can see that you are a prophet. Our fathers worshiped on this mountain, but you Jews claim that the place where we must worship is in Jerusalem."

Jesus declared, "Believe me, woman, a time is coming when you will worship the Father neither on this mountain nor in Jerusalem. You Samaritans worship what you do not know; we worship what we do know, for salvation is from the Jews. Yet a time is coming and has now come when the true worshipers will worship the Father in spirit and truth, for they are the kind of worshipers the Father seeks. God is spirit, and His worshipers must worship in spirit and in truth." The woman said, "I know that Messiah" (called Christ) "is coming. When he comes, he will explain everything to us." John 4:15-25

These opening words, "Sir, give me this water so that I won't get thirsty and have to keep coming here to draw water," have received varied and almost conflicting interpretations. We dismiss at once, as unsatisfactory, that which would represent them as the expression of a childlike faith, a further development in the woman's dawning convictions, which were soon to culminate in perfect unwavering belief. Two other interpretations appear alone to be tenable. Her answer may have been simply dictated by stupid, ignorant wonder; it may have been the utterance of a carnal, sensuous heart, dull and dead to all spiritual apprehension—unable, as we have already seen, to rise above earthly things, or to extract any higher meaning from the sublime and gracious declaration of the stranger than a poor material reference to the well at her feet, and the economy of time and toil in being relieved of the necessity to "keep coming here to draw water."

An alternative interpretation is perhaps more in harmony alike with the woman's character and with the tenor of the narrative, that is, that her response was neither the dictate of wonder nor of faith, but rather an attempt, by evasion and banter, to trifle with divine realities—that it was uttered in a sarcastic, frivolous spirit, in a tone of playful irony. As if she had said, purposely to evade the spiritual application, 'Yes, truly, this mythical living water of yours *would* be a good thing indeed! it would really be worth knowing and having. Lord, give me this water, that I thirst not, neither keep coming here to draw water.'

She had, it is true, in an earlier part of the conversation, given promise of better things. She had seemed, at all events, impressed with the unwonted courtesy of this Jerusalem Pilgrim, and to have reciprocated it. But the impression, on a heart in which pride and sin were dominant, was only momentary—the wave only touched the living rock to retreat back again amid the eddying waters. The old nature and the defiant tone return and resume the mastery. She petulantly spurns a style of discourse at variance with the whole current of her carnal thoughts and carnal life. She has no belief in, no patience for, such serious talk as this. Her answer is in the taunting, skeptical, scornful spirit of the scoffers in Ezekiel's time, "Ah, Lord God, they say of me, Does he not speak parables?"

Although of comparatively little importance which interpretation we select, we are inclined to think that the latter is most in consonance with the immediately subsequent dealing which our Lord deems it necessary to employ. When He thus saw that she was trifling, or affecting to trifle, with the profoundest needs of her soul, He resorts to the use of strong means in order to rouse her from her apathy, and guilt, and awful peril. 'The wind, and the earthquake, and the fire' must follow 'the still small voice.'

He therefore breaks off the conversation abruptly, and pursues a new theme. There is nothing more said now in connection with the beautiful similitude of the well and the living water. If she cannot be approached by imagery and figure, He will come home to her hardened conscience by the use of facts from which there can be no escape. She may misunderstand and misinterpret symbolic teaching, but there can be no misunderstanding about the stern and sad realities of her own life. He drags to view her besetting sin. Suddenly terminating the figurative conversation, he sends home this arrow of conviction, "Go, call your husband, and come here!"

In a light, bravado spirit—the reflection of her character and history—she replies, with no sense of shame or sorrow, "I have no husband." Or, it may be, ignorant of the omniscient Being she confronted, who then read the blotted pages of her heart, she tried to *evade the truth* by the utterance of a lie. But she was soon convinced that He in whose presence she stood, was one 'from whom no secrets are hidden'—the discerner of the thoughts and the intents of the heart. In one brief sentence He unfolds a terrible life-story with its crowning act of present guilt. "Jesus said unto her, You have well said, I have no husband, for you have had five husbands, and he whom you now have is not your husband; in that said you truly."

We might have supposed that after this, evasion was impossible; that, as the timid bird cowers under the glance of the falcon or the eagle, so would this convicted sinner have trembled under the revelations of that infinitely pure One, who, from the deep well of her polluted life, had drawn up the evidences of impurity and debasement; and that casting herself convicted and condemned at the feet of her Divine Censor, she would have exclaimed, "Have you found me, O my enemy?"

The barbed arrow indeed could not fail to reach its mark; but even now, as it pierces her seared conscience, she makes a bold and adroit attempt to turn the subject—to evade the scrutiny. This she tries to effect by a twofold deception. The first only of these two efforts, and the manner in which our Lord meets it, we shall be able to examine in this chapter.

By a dexterous shift and diversion she starts a controversial topic. It is only those who have stood by the actual spot, with all the old, unchanged surroundings of the Well of Jacob, who can fully realize and picture the scene, as, pointing upwards to the heights of the sacred mountain close by, she exclaimed, "Sir, I perceive that you are a prophet. Our fathers worshiped in this mountain, and you say that in Jerusalem is the place where men ought to worship." She had already, in the context, adverted to religious differences—the old feud existing between Jew and Samaritan. She had passed from that, to historical and ancestral questions regarding Father Jacob. Now she invites discussion on the controversy between the rival temples of Gerizim and Zion, and their comparative claims to superior sanctity.

What does this teach; but how possible it is to talk fluently on controversial themes, to start speculative questions—points of religious debate—to fight sectarian battles, defend to the death every letter of party shibboleth, exclaiming, "The temple of the Lord, the temple of the Lord, the temple of the Lord are we," *and yet to live godless lives.* Here was one; not only outraging the laws of heaven and earth, but also utterly indifferent to her own abandoned career; and yet, apparently with a martyr's heroism, she enters the lists as a sectary; she could speak readily on semi-religious questions; she could talk, with all the fiery zeal of a partisan, of "our fathers," and gloried in being a separatist from the tribe of Judah.

Picture, alas! of multitudes still, who are living in deepest ignorance of their own guilt and danger, their corruption in heart and life; who are yet great champions in some denominational battlefield; who, with stern self-isolation, entrench themselves in sectarian pride and formalism—blow loud the trumpet of religious partisanship; valiant athletes in some debatable question of creed and sect, plying their weapons with untiring ingenuity so long as the *personal and practical issues* can be evaded and eliminated; very tolerant of their own frailties, but very intolerant of the frailties and short-comings of others—loyalty to party, usurping the place the gospel assigns to charity, in covering a multitude of sins. Such, then, was the woman of Samaria's first attempt at evasion.

Let us listen now to the Savior's memorable reply; the order of which, for the better elucidation of the meaning, we may somewhat transpose. He first gives a bold and decided answer to her question, and then grounds upon it some grand truths, whose comfort and consolation were intended for all ages of the future. To her query as to the rival claims of Mount Gerizim and Zion, He affirms, without hesitation, the orthodoxy of the *Jewish* and the heterodoxy of the *Samaritan* worship: "You worship you know not what; we know what we worship, for salvation is of the Jews." He thus unflinchingly condemns the defectiveness of the Samaritan creed—their rejection of the entire succession of inspired prophets, as well as their partial toleration of the half heathen ceremonies which had been incorporated in the worship of the God of Israel on Gerizim. By assimilating their religious ceremonial to the rites of Phoenicia and Greece, they had practically set up an altar with the inscription, "To the Unknown God."

Moreover, Zion being the appointed city of solemnities where the tribes were to go up, they were guilty of breaking, unsanctioned, the old historic unity of worship. On the other hand, Jesus adds, as Himself of the tribe of Judah, "We know what we worship." The Jews were the divinely accredited custodians of the truth; "Unto them were committed the oracles of God." Apostate, in one sense, as the worshipers on Zion had become from the living faith of their forefathers, they at all events retained intact and unmutilated their monotheism, as well as the ancient Mosaic and Levitical institutions. Along with the Pentateuch, they reverenced the authority of the prophetic voices which age after age had been preparing the way for the new Gospel era. They were uncorrupted by Baal worship. The temple courts were undesecrated by the arts of the magician and necromancer. More than that, "Salvation" (literally, in the original, "the Salvation," or, as some would render it, "the Savior," the promised Messiah, "is of the Jews." Of them, as concerning the flesh, Christ was to come. From the tribe of Judah, not from Ephraim, He was to spring.

The fountain opened for sin and for uncleanness was, in the first instance, "for the house of David and for the inhabitants of Jerusalem." The Lord had chosen Jerusalem as the place to put His name there. Ezekiel's living waters, emblematic of Gospel grace and blessing, were to go forth from the Temple of Zion to refresh and fertilize earth's waste places—the moral wildernesses of humanity. No, farther, not without note and significance is the tense of the word here employed. It is not "the Salvation" *shall be*, but *"is,"* of the Jews, probably indicating to the listener that that Savior or "Salvation" had already appeared, and thus forming a preparation for the more distinct and unqualified assurance which follows, when He declares Himself, without reserve, to be the promised Messiah.

But having thus unhesitatingly vindicated the claims of Jerusalem and Zion, He at the same time announces two truths of world-wide interest, regarding alike the *object* of worship and the *manner* of worship. We may invert also the order in which these stand in the narrative. As to the OBJECT of worship, He gives to this ignorant woman a revelation of the Supreme Being under two distinct aspects—

(1.) "God is a SPIRIT," or "God is spirit." He may, in her case, have had a double reason for thus adverting to the immaterial nature of Jehovah. Material forms, as we have previously mentioned, had been sanctioned in the compound mongrel-worship on Gerizim, in accommodation to the tastes and propensities of the heathen colonists—forms that were of necessity *localized,* and which were supposed to exercise no influence save in the vicinity of their shrine or temple. Moreover, the pure faith had been farther corrupted by combining with this material, a spurious spirit-worship. The votaries of Baal had a spirit presiding over the scenes and elements of nature—woods and mountains, fire, air, and water. Jesus reveals the glorious truth, of which this latter was the debasing counterfeit.

God is a *spirit*. Not a *local* God, restricted to that neighboring hill; but the Great Universal—not presiding over any favorite haunt or segment of the globe, but according to the beautiful description of one of those Psalms which the Samaritan had rejected, "If I ascend up into heaven, You are there. If I make my bed in hell, behold You are there. If I take the wings of the morning, and dwell in the uttermost parts of the sea, even there shall Your hand lead me, and Your right hand shall hold me." In opposition to spirit-worship—the false teaching of their magicians and enchanters—here was the glorious unseen reality. These *spirits*, supposed by some of them to haunt the woods and groves and streamlets of Gerizim, or, in demon form to take possession of the human soul—were the phantoms of their own brain, the forms of a credulous superstition. But here with the Jews, was the only true (the Omnipresent) Spirit, who needed no temples made with hands.

And, yet once more, the Samaritan worship, either of the material symbol or of the local spirit, had become a *heartless form*. Religion had degenerated into the most worthless and debasing ritualism—a round of externals, in which true worship, the worship of the heart and the obedience of the life, had no place. Not so was it in the worship of this spiritual Jehovah. "Those who worship Him must worship Him in spirit and in truth." Thus, then, the Savior's declaration was a needed counteractive to false views on *the great elementary truth of all religious creeds—the nature of the Supreme Object of worship.*

This woman may have been conversant, probably from infancy, with some of these strange, extravagant beliefs in a spirit-world. She had been surrounded by lying prophets, and credited their lying wonders. Christ directs her to the true spirit-worship. "You worship you know not what."—You have conjured up a spirit-land and a dream-land which have no existence. But I now reveal to you the great truth you have overlaid by your demonology, and desecrated by your practice: "God is a spirit, AND those who worship Him must worship Him in spirit and in truth.

(2.) He makes a second and still more glorious—still more novel and startling revelation of the nature and name of the Supreme Being. God as a FATHER. "The Father." It was a new name—a new apocalypse of the Almighty Ruler of her nation. She had just spoken in sectarian pride of "our fathers," and of Father Jacob. In emphatic contrast with this, Jesus can tell of the true Father—the eternal Father—the Father of His universal Church and people. It was a name, not indeed unknown in the books of the Jewish prophets, but it was a name which specially belonged to the new and dawning Gospel dispensation. "The hour, (that is, the Gospel hour), comes, and now is, when the true worshipers shall worship the Father."

The woman of Sychar had done foul dishonor to other most sacred ties of earth. Could no muffled harp-string in her soul wake up in trembling melody, as to an old familiar strain, by the mention of this new name? Debased as she now was, might she not, amid the memories of childhood-innocence, recall the hour when she loved to lisp that word? Amid the wreck of all other human relationships, might she not think of, and cling kindly to, the oldest and tenderest of all?

God was such to her—God was her Father—that universal Spirit was the universal Parent of all who worshiped Him in spirit and in truth. The thought would bring Him near as He never was before. It would invest Him with a new attractiveness. It would unteach in a moment many of the falsities of the Baal creed; and specially, its tendency to cause the Jehovah of Israel to be regarded with repulsiveness and terror—a Being of wrath to be appeased, but not of love or beauty in whom affection and trust might repose.

Of this Almighty Parent, Jesus adds, "the Father seeks such to worship Him." May not these words have further endeared to her His new name? The term "seeks" is not in the sense of 'wishes' or 'desires,' but of going after, to search and find. It is the Shepherd "seeking his flock that are scattered in the cloudy and dark day." "Behold I, even I, will both search my sheep and find them out." Was she not one of that scattered flock, the worst truant of all the fold? The Shepherd was seeking her—or rather, that Old Testament figure and simile is superseded by the more touching Gospel symbol, "The Father" seeks his prodigal child—yes, and the Father waits not in his palace halls for the wanderer's return, but he goes forth on his mission of parental love. New and glorious step in the ladder by which she was brought up out of the horrible pit and the miry clay!

'Father, my Father;' 'He seeks me.' That earthly name, as we have just said, may have been to her, a fading remembrance. One of the rocky sepulchers at the base of Gerizim may now have been all that could recall it; and she may have felt thankful that he who claimed the relationship had not lived to see it disgraced in her own immoral life. But the old and hallowed earthly tie may be revived in a new and more enduring form. The God of Gerizim, the God of Israel, the God of Abraham and Isaac and Jacob—He is my Father. I may cry unto Him, "You are my Father, my God, and the Rock of my salvation."

If unable yet to grasp the blessed truth, she came before long to do so. Perhaps long after this interview was over, she may have lived to read in future years, in a letter from one, who, like herself, was a monument of Redeeming grace and divine parental love, "I will receive you, and will be a Father unto you, and you shall be my sons and daughters, says the Lord Almighty." (2 Cor. 6:18)

But it is not only a revelation of the Supreme object of worship the Redeemer makes to the woman of Sychar. He has an equally glorious and important revelation as to the PLACE AND MANNER OF WORSHIP. "Jesus said unto her, Woman, believe me, the hour comes when you shall neither in this mountain, nor at Jerusalem worship the Father," (or rather, "not in this mountain only, nor in Jerusalem, you shall worship the Father.") All *local* worship is to terminate; all old things are to pass away, and all things are to be made new. Hitherto, under a preparatory dispensation, God had chosen out a people for Himself. Jerusalem had been His earthly audience-chamber, the repository of the true faith; the mystic cloud, the symbol of Deity, had rested in the holy of holies within Zion's temple. But the *Gospel hour* has now dawned, the substance has come, and the shadows are fleeing away. Soon the symbolic veil of that Temple shall be rent, intimating not only the abolition and abrogation of all ceremonial worship, but the extinction of all exclusive religious localities, privileged "holy places"— the inauguration of an era of worldwide blessing—the brotherhood of the nations under the one universal Spirit—a church gathered out of every country, under one Father.

The Great Shepherd will go forth, not as of old, on the mountains of Judah or Israel, but out amid earth's pathless wastes, from distant east to distant west, wherever the lost and the wandering are to be found. And no one spot in all the vast circuit will be more sacred than another. Gerizim—that boasted "mountain of blessing" is now to give its name to the whole earth. "In all places where I record my name, I will come unto you and bless you." The round globe, with the blue vault of heaven for its canopy, will henceforth form the stupendous temple of the great Unseen and Invisible. The true and accepted Israel—the "Father-worshipers," will be found in every corner of the habitable world—in those glorious climates of the sun where idolatry has long reigned with undisputed sway—where the mosque and the pagoda have for ages frowned defiance on the Christian sanctuary—in the distant isles of the ocean—amid the prairies and pastures of the far west, the arid sands of the tropics—or amid the icebergs of eternal winter— yes, and not more under the gorgeous church or fretted aisle, than

in the crude garret of the city, the humble hovel of the country, the
secluded cavern of the mountain, the pathless forest of the settler,
the solitary craft or deck of the fisherman and seaman, the lonely
chamber of the poor, the sick, the bedridden, the dying—

"Wherever they seek You, You are found,
And every place is hallowed ground."

The woman of Samaria pointed, with the pride of sect and tribe,
to the *locality* as if that were everything. But, in His brief answer,
Jesus proclaims the great truth, that the locality is nothing. The
material offering was unimportant, but the acceptable and grateful
incense to this Great Spirit and Father was the fragrance of a broken heart and a holy life. All outward symbols, Gerizim and Zion,
and their conflicting claims, are to be merged in the sanctities of
a nobler temple, an inner shrine—"You are the temple of the Holy
Spirit." "The temple of the Lord is holy, which temple you are."

Among other solemn and urgent lessons these magnificent utterances bring home to us, surely one is, the duty, not only of
moderating the wild excess of religious exclusiveness, but the folly
of putting *external forms* on the same level or platform with *eternal
principles of faith and obedience*. When will men take down this
complicated scaffolding which obscures and obstructs the grand
proportions of the Temple of Truth? When will the sun arise to
quench these fires of our own kindling? When will the material
give way to the spiritual; the human and the incidental to the divine and the everlasting? When will individuals and Churches, as
the children of one redeemed family, come, in childlike faith and
childlike love, to worship 'the Father?'

What a different world would this be, did these two eternal
words—eternal 'articles'—assert their glorious sway, and be allowed to perform their limitless errand! "God is a SPIRIT"—this
is the first and fundamental teaching of the missionary in over-
turning all idolatries and gross material forms and sensuous worship—demanding 'spirit and truth,' purity and earnestness, the
homage of the heart and the consecration of the life. "God is a
FATHER"—this is the Gospel's precious and consolatory message
to the prodigal, the disinherited, the lost.

Do we know the preciousness—do we ponder alike the solemnity
and the consolation, of this twofold name? God is a SPIRIT! How
soul-stirring, how awe-inspiring would be the habitual recollec-
tion of this simplest but truly greatest of elementary truths; that
that august Being, that Great unseen, unknown, untraceable, in-

tangible—is everywhere present, beneath, around, about me—the witness of all my actions, with the eye of unerring scrutiny searching the secret labyrinths of my heart! "Where shall I go from your spirit, or where shall I flee from your presence?"

God is my FATHER! The feeling of *awe* encompassing the Supreme Spirit melts into *affection*. The cloud and the darkness resolve themselves into a halo of softened tenderness. That all-seeing One is the prototype of the dearest of human relations—the earthly parent is the shadowy image of the heavenly. "The Father"—but it is the Father *in Christ the Son*; "My Father," and therefore "your Father." Not the Father of *universal humanity*, that modern travesty of the true Fatherhood of God—but the Father of that redeemed humanity which has its representative elder Brother now before the throne, and who gives, in one glorious sentence, the condition and qualification of sonship: "As many as received Him, to them gave He power (the right) to become the sons of God, even to those who believe on His name." "If you knew the gift of God, and who it is that says unto you, Give me to drink, you would have asked of Him, and He would have given you living water."

Could the revelation of the God of Christianity, the God of the Gospel go no farther than this? Yes; yet another name and title of the Almighty, flowing from this paternal relation, was reserved for one of these apostles (who had now gone into the city to buy food,) subsequently to unfold to believers and the Church. This woman of Samaria, now groping in the darkness, may, too, have one day read in his epistles, its letters of living light. With it, the evolution of the Divine character terminates. Heaven knows no more—can give no more. The archangel can climb no higher. It is the loftiest expression of the august Fatherhood; and Jesus leaves it to the lips, we may reverently say, next best qualified to His own to pronounce it: "God is LOVE."

This bright pinnacle of faith—this third and last step in the golden ladder, may we also be enabled to reach. Rising in the sublime gradation, may it be ours to grasp the threefold name—that trinity of divine attributes, with all their elevating motives and everlasting consolations. The triple theme of meditation in the Church on earth, it will form the triple theme of adoring contemplation and immortal praise in the Church of the glorified—

God is a SPIRIT,
God is a FATHER,
God is LOVE!

SECOND EVASION AND REPLY

The woman said, "I know that Messiah" (called Christ) "is coming. When he comes, he will explain everything to us."

Then Jesus declared, "I who speak to you am he." John 4:25-26

In the previous chapter we considered the first means employed by the unknown and unrecognized Heart-searcher to rouse the dulled, torpid conscience of the woman of Samaria. We considered the evasive answer which she gave to the unexpected revelation of her flagrant life, by attempting to *divert the conversation to a controversial topic* about the competing claims of Mounts Gerizim and Zion. This in its turn drew forth our Lord's sublime reply, in which He announced the abrogation of all ceremonial worship, the abolition of all distinctive "holy places," the establishment of a universal Church, and proclaimed Israel's God under a new gospel name, setting forth His *paternal* relation to His believing people—"The Church throughout all the world does acknowledge you, THE FATHER of an infinite majesty!"

We might have expected, after the gracious and impressive words which had thus proceeded out of His mouth, (beginning with the condescending offer of the living water, passing to the prophetic cognizance of her heart and life history, and ending with the revelation of the divine Fatherhood,) that she would at once have bowed in lowly humility before Him, confessing her sin—recognizing one who, with divine intuition, "understood her errors," saying, "Cleanse me from secret faults;" at the same time adding, in a very different spirit from that in which it was first uttered, "Lord, give me this water, that I thirst not."

But not so. The *stricken deer* tries once more to wrench the rankling arrow from the wound. The *lost wanderer of the fold*, thus caught amid the entangling thorns, makes yet one other effort to escape from the arms of the pursuing shepherd. Or, dropping all figure, *this bold transgressor*, unable to discuss these spiritual themes which her Lord had just been unfolding, tries to stifle her convictions by the new plea of procrastination. "I know that Messiah who is called Christ is coming. When he comes, he will explain everything to us."—'He will tell us all these things of which you have now been speaking—He will decide all controversies; He will settle all rival claims; He will unfold to us these deep and glorious mysteries about the nature and the name of God, and regarding the Church of the future.' She wished apparently with this, to break off and silence the conversation, and in the spirit of a later conscience-stricken sinner, to say, "Go your way for this time; when I have a convenient season, I will call for you."

PROCRASTINATION, in its Proteus shapes, is the most effectual and the most fatal device which Satan has in every age employed for luring unwary and unthinking thousands to destruction. Postponing the great question of salvation to this indefinite convenient season, the cry of the convicted soul is, "Give me this water!"—but not yet.

"Give me this water!" is the cry of *youth*—but not yet. Disturb not my bright sunny morning; wait until I reach the threshold of manhood.

"Give me this water!" is the cry of ripening *manhood*—but not yet. Disturb me not in the burden and heat of the day; wait until I have leisure and breathing-time; wait until the eventide sets in, and the shadows are lengthening, and the drawers of water stand with their pitchers around life's fountains.

"Give me this water!" is the cry of *old age*—but not yet. Though far advanced in the pilgrimage journey, my strength is yet firm. I have a long evening before the sunset hour. I may linger yet a while amid these olive-glades, before the flagon be let down for the draught.

"Give me this water!" is the cry of the *dying*. But postponement cannot be pled now; procrastination merges into despair. "Give me this water!" but it is too late. It must now be an unresponded-to call. These tottering steps cannot now bear me to the well's brink; these feeble hands are unable to grasp the pitcher and quench this deathless thirst.

Oh, Procrastination! how many has your siren voice *lulled, and beguiled, and ruined!* How true, if it be quaint, is the well-known saying of an old divine—the sad verity it describes redeems it from triteness or commonplace—that "Hell is paved with good intentions;" or, as this is expressed in another form, in one of the sententious lines of the poet of "Night Thoughts"—

"Men resolve, and re-resolve, then die the same."

But to return to the narrative. Although such was the woman's dexterous new expedient to divert and terminate the conversation, she could hardly fail to have had other conflicting thoughts also in

that most momentous hour of her existence. In her very attempts
at evasion, she could not shake off altogether the conviction, that
she was standing in the presence of a superior Being; one who
had unmasked her inner life, laid bare her ignominious past. She
owns him as "a prophet." He had spoken in authoritative accents;
His sayings were as strange as they were impressive. If she was
perplexed and staggered at the similitude He had employed about
"living water," and "everlasting life," still more unconventional
were His earnest, commanding, arresting, comforting words—
"Believe *Me*" "The hour now is" "The Father (whose lost child you
are) seeks," and seeks *you*. He had, moreover, pointedly adverted
(verse 22) to "the salvation," or "the Savior."

She remembered the great tradition of her nation. A nobler life
and hope and reality, indeed, this tradition was to the neighboring
Jews, whose sacred writings were full of predictions of a mighty
coming Deliverer. But their own venerated Pentateuch had inspired the same expectations. The Jews looked for the Messiah
as a great temporal King; but the one prophecy of Moses was in
true harmony with her present reference to the Messiah-hope as
a *Teacher*—"When He has come, He will tell us (or teach us) all
things." "The Lord your God," was the remarkable Pentateuch pre-
diction, "will raise up unto you a Prophet from the midst of you, of
your brethren, like unto me—unto Him you shall hearken."

When she listened, therefore, with arrested ear and smitten soul
to the divine utterances of this mysterious Jewish Rabbi, may not
the thought possibly have flashed vaguely across her mind, min-
gling with her defiant unbelief, and with her real or pretended
evasions, "Can this be Him?" It must be remembered that not the
dwellers in Palestine only, but the nations of the world were, at
this epoch, in dreamy expectation of some divine advent or incar-
nation. Across on those Trans-Jordanic hills on which she could
gaze from where she stood through the opening of the valley, a
strange prophetic voice had, fifteen hundred years before, taken
up the parable with which her own Pentateuch may have made
her familiar—"I see Him, but not in the present time. I perceive
Him, but far in the distant future. A Star will rise from Jacob;
a Scepter will emerge from Israel. It will crush the foreheads of
Moab's people, cracking the skulls of the people of Sheth."

The caravans of travelers, passing daily Jacob's Well on the
high road to Galilee, must have deepened these anticipations by
their tidings of the marvelous preacher of the Jewish desert—"the
voice crying in the wilderness." That voice, indeed, had in thrilling

words announced the very truths to which she had now been the strange auditor—"Prepare the way of the Lord, make His paths straight. Every valley shall be filled, and every mountain and hill shall be brought low; and the crooked shall be made straight, and the rough ways shall be made smooth; and all flesh shall see the salvation of God."

And what was to her more arresting far than these general prophetic hopes, He who now addressed her had roused her slumbering conscience—the arrow was sticking fast there. If he had not "told her all things," He had, at all events, vindicated His claims to her attention and reverence by an irresistible argument—He had told her about **herself**. She could not stifle these aroused convictions. To use Chrysostom's quaint but emphatic words, she must have been "made dizzy with Christ's discourse." It was the crisis-moment in her spiritual history; verily but a step between either life or death. Guilty caviler that she was, who knew not the time of her visitation—meeting overtures of grace with evasion after evasion—it might have been said of her as of the tribe of Ephraim to which she belonged, She is "joined to her idols, let her alone!"

Is the divine Savior, whose forbearance she has thus been trifling and tampering with, to *abandon her to her procrastination and unbelief and cherished sins?* or, by one bold and gracious answer, will He lift the curtain from the glories of His divine Person, as it had not yet been lifted either in Galilee or Judea? Such a premature disclosure of His Messiah claims may be fraught with peril and disadvantage, seeing that His hour had not yet come. But the destinies of one human soul are suspended on that revelation; He will save others, not save Himself. If the inward sigh of her burdened heart corresponded with that of the Greek Gentiles at a later period, "Sir, we would see Jesus!" the glad and astounding response is now given from the living oracle—"Jesus said unto her, *I who speak unto you am He.*"

What an unexpected rejoinder to her recent question, "Are you greater than our father Jacob?" 'Yes!' is His reply, 'I am greater. I am the Shiloh of whom he spoke. I am the true ladder he beheld in mystic vision on yonder heights of Bethel, by which the guilty can climb to the heaven they have forfeited and the God they have offended!' The triumph is complete. The darkness is past, and the true light shines—"I am He!" It is enough. The Baptist's bold words, uttered on the neighboring banks of the Jordan, have now their first echo and fulfillment at the base of Gerizim, "Whose fan is in his hand, and he will thoroughly purge his floor, and will *gather the wheat into his garner."*

Whatever had been her prejudices, her sectarian bitterness, her sarcasm, her evasions, she re-traverses at a glance the glowing words of the conversation. She understands all now. The kindness, the grace, the truth, the penetrating revelations of Omniscience, the strange urgency and earnestness, the living water, salvation, everlasting life. HE, the great Giver of all, is standing by her side, and offering these priceless blessings to her! yes, to her with her legion-sins—the demon-throng that had reigned unchallenged for long years in her degraded heart. She asks, she needs no outer sign. He had told her 'all things that ever she did.' She requires no attesting angels to gather around the well—no horses and chariots of fire on Gerizim, as of old on the mountain at Dothan, to authenticate His mission.

The pilgrim garb the Traveler wears, and the signs of weariness and languor, cannot in her eyes belie His claims to be the true Messiah. The "follow me," which had acted with omnipotent spell on the fishermen at Bethsaida, had fallen with like irresistible energy on her own soul. She heard, she listened, she repented, she believed, she rejoiced! She has already let down her pitcher for the draught, and feels as if for the first time that her deep spiritual thirst was quenched forever.

The sequel is unrecorded. Whether she fell prostrate adoring at His feet, exclaiming, with Thomas, "My Lord and my God," we cannot tell. Her feelings at that moment are left to our imagination. Very possibly there was nothing more for the evangelist to note. She may have been dumb with *silence*, unable to utter a word—dumb, it may be, with *tears*.

Already, too, the disciples are appearing from the city amid the olive-glades with their purchased food. But as we see this now saved one hastening with buoyant step on her mission of wonder and gratitude and joy to her native town, we can imagine the heart-song which the lips failed to embody in utterance—"I will praise You, O Lord my God, with all my heart, and I will glorify Your name for evermore, for great is Your mercy towards me, and You have delivered my soul from the lowest hell!"

"Likewise, I say unto you, there is joy in the presence of the angels of God over one sinner that repents."

Let us come once more, at this climax of the story, and admire and adore *the riches of redeeming grace and love.* Behold Christ standing at the door of a closed heart, still waiting and knocking in wondrous patience and forbearance, though His head be wet with dew, and His locks with the drops of the night, until the response was heard, "Come in, O blessed of the Lord; why do you stand outside?" It was truly predicted of Him, "The bruised reed He will not break; the smoking flax he will not quench, until he bring forth judgment unto victory."

Seated as He now was at that well-side amid the mountains of Ephraim, His own words, uttered aforetime by the mouth of His prophet, had a new and significant interpretation: "Oh, how can I give you up, Israel? How can I let you go? How can I destroy you like Admah and Zeboiim? My heart is torn within me, and my compassion overflows. No, I will not punish you as much as my burning anger tells me to. I will not completely destroy Israel, for I am God and not a mere mortal. I am the Holy One living among you, and I will not come to destroy." The lesson may well be engraven as with an iron pen and lead on these rocks forever, that none need despair—that the first may be last, and the last first; that for *Samaritan* sinners, as for *Jerusalem* sinners, there is mercy. The vilest prodigal may come and read the superscription on the well of Jacob: "This is a faithful saying, and worthy of all acceptance, that Jesus Christ came into the world to save sinners, of whom I am chief." That day *salvation* had come to her house. As the first fruits of Israel's ingathering, the longing aspiration of the great Psalmist prophet was fulfilled, "Oh that the Salvation (or the Savior) of Israel were come out of Zion! When the Lord brings back the captivity of His people, Jacob shall rejoice, and Israel shall be glad."

"I who speak unto you," said Jesus to the woman. Christ is speaking to us in many ways. He speaks in the mercies He bestows, and in the blessings He withholds; in life's storms and life's sunshine; in the earthquake and the fire, as well as in the still small voice. "I who speak unto you." That is His utterance, if we would but hear it, in the midst of our worldly losses—our desolate homes—our sickbeds—our deathbeds.

Blessed be God, too, as in the case of the woman of Samaria, He has one louder utterance still: "I who speak in righteousness— mighty to save!" Never is there the season, or the exigency, in which He is unable or unwilling to reveal Himself. During his ministry on earth, He seemed as if He would make every hour take up its parable as to His readiness at all times thus to "speak peace to His people and to His saints." Early in the *morning*, before the sun had risen on the hills of Bashan, He spoke to His disciples on the lake-shores of Galilee. At *midday*—with the glaring sun in the meridian—He met this sinful woman at the well of Jacob. At *eventide*, on the way to Emmaus, when His disciples were indulging in sorrowful musings about their absent Lord, the mysterious stranger who joined their company said to them, "I who speak unto you am He." At *night*, when all was hushed in Jerusalem, He spoke comfortable words to Nicodemus. Or on the *sea* of Gennesaret, when, amid darkness and tempest, the disciples, like this woman of Samaria, failed to recognize their divine Master—when they could see nothing but an evil spirit (as they surmised, a demon of the deep) walking on the crested waves, the voice was heard, "It is I; do not be afraid!"

And if we take all these as *symbolic of the varied hours in life's little day*, Jesus speaks in each of them. *Youth!* in life's early morning, the dawn of existence, He speaks to you. *Manhood* and womanhood! at the well-side, in the hot noon of life, He speaks to you. *Old-age!* in life's evening, in mellowed sundown, He speaks to you. *Dying!* out in the midst of the cold dark sea, death coming in spirit-form, and extracting at first the cry of fear—He speaks to you in the gentle accents of His own love.

Has He spoken to us? Like that woman at the well at Sychar, that poor wandering bird of Samaria, long having no resting-place for the sole of our feet, have we found it at last in the true Ark? Have we listened to the gracious revelation, I am He? Have we listened to these balm-words which fell of old on the ears of other similar outcasts—"Come unto me, all you who labor and are heavy laden, and I will give you rest?"

It is said of Goethe, the great German, that in one of those dark unsatisfied hours in which his mighty intellect and soul groped after the true rest, he thus recorded his undefined longings for that which he had failed to attain—

Fairest among Heaven's daughters,
You who stillest pain and woe,
Pour Your refreshing waters
On the thirsty here below;
Where tends this restless striving!
Faint and tired I long for rest.
Heaven-born Peace,
Come and dwell within my breast!"

These words were found on a scrap of paper lying on his writing-table. A devoted friend of kindred intellectual pursuits, but who had tasted of a better fountain and therefore knew what alone could quench these unsated aspirations, wrote on the other side, "Peace I leave with you, my peace I give unto you. Let not your heart be troubled, neither let it be afraid."

"If you knew the GIFT OF GOD and who it is that asks you for a drink, you would have asked Him and HE would have given you living water." And if we would add yet one word, it is that Christ, in the glories of His person and offices and work, as revealed here and elsewhere in the Gospels, with His free message of salvation, is the very Savior we need, and who alone can satisfy the soul's thirst. Christianity is to have no new phases or developments. Its glorious distinctive truths are not to be molded and metamorphosed to suit the restless spirit of the times, to adapt themselves to new conditions of thought, and to square with modern theories and speculations. Jesus, from being the adorable God-man, "Immanuel, God with us," is not to be dishonored by merely having a place assigned Him as one of many deities in the world's Pantheon—regarded simply as the human Founder of one of earth's religions or philosophies—and the doctrines of His school to take complexion and color, shape and modification, at the caprice of human opinion—the age molding the gospel instead of the gospel molding the age. Poetry is at fault when this is one of her oracular utterances, "Ring in the Christ that is to be."

The Christ that 'is to be' is the Christ that *is*. "I who speak unto you am He." "They shall perish," may be true of all other philosophic creeds and systems, "but You remain the same." "Jesus Christ the same yesterday, and today, and forever."

May *we* know Him as the unchanging Savior, the Giver of the living water, the Speaker of peace, the Bestower of rest to the soul. Renouncing and loathing our sins, and having had answered in Him the cry of thirsting humanity, "Give me to drink!"—may we be able to say, with holy earnestness and believing joy,

"Is there a thing beneath the sun
That strives with You my heart to share;
Ah, take it thence, and reign alone,
The Lord of every motive there.
Then shall my heart from earth be free,
When it has found repose in Thee!"

MOMENTS OF SILENCE

"Just then his disciples arrived. They were astonished to find him talking to a woman, but none of them asked him why he was doing it or what they had been discussing." John 4:27

Sacred story has on record many crisis-hours of thrilling interest. Such was the occasion when the old Judge of Israel sat by the wayside 'trembling for the ark of God'—when the liberties of his country, the safety of the sacred symbol of which he was custodian, and the fate of his own family, were all involved in the momentous issues of the struggle. Such, too, was the kindred occasion when David sat in an agony of suspense between the two gates when the battle was raging in the woods of Ephraim, and when, with parental feelings triumphing over the larger interests at stake, he inquired in eager and anxious haste, "Is the young man Absalom safe?"

Few among ourselves, doubtless, in our individual histories, have not known of similar seasons—when the telegraph flashed its unexpected message of the distant *bereavement*, or the *appalling accident*; or when in our own home we watched the herald symptoms of dissolution gathering round some loved pillow—'life balanced in a breath'—when hope and fear had for long days their alternate triumph, and when the unmistakable indication was given by skilled watchers, which quick-sighted affection too well understands, that recovery was hopeless.

Or, to take the converse of these; many doubtless can recall experiences of a different kind—life's gladder recollections—bright milestones and way-marks in the pilgrimage—momentous events enshrined in sunny memories—the birth of a child—the return of a long-absent son or brother from a far-off land—the first success in business—the triumph in some struggle of honorable ambition; or, it may be, the electric message which conveyed the cheering intelligence that the illness and danger of our friend was over, or that he had come unscathed out of the fiery tide of battle, or was rescued safe from some perishing crew. These, and such like, which each separate experience doubtless has to suggest, form the "illi dies" of the old Roman—days which he was used to mark with the white or black chalk, the symbols of joy or sorrow.

But what season can be compared in its momentousness to the great crisis-hour of a **soul's conversion**; an hour similar to that which we contemplated in the preceding context—the triumph of light over darkness—truth over error—life over death? What return so glad as the return of the long lost prodigal to the heavenly Father's home? What day so deservedly to be marked with the white chalk of gladness as the day which *records the soul's deliverance from everlasting danger and ruin?* What birth compared to that of an heir of immortality?

Is it to be wondered at, that such momentous epochs of our earthly histories as those of which we have spoken, should, at the instant of their occurrence thrill the spirit into silence? that the tongue in such seasons of agitating emotion should be unable to speak—that utterance should fail?

Is it a time of *grief, overpowering sorrow?* That word "overpowering" expresses our meaning—the lips at the moment refuse to tell out the secrets of the speechless, stricken, smitten heart. Sorrow is always deepest, profoundest, where the mourners can exchange only silent glances through irrepressible tears. Job's three friends, when they heard of his aggravated woes, sat along with him upon the ground with torn mantle and dust-covered heads for seven days and seven nights, "and none," we read, "spoke a word unto him, for they saw that his grief was very great."

Or, is it some *joyful occasion?* Joy has its strange, stunning moment, too. The receipt of sudden and gladdening information has been known, for the time being, to paralyze into silence the overstrung feelings, to hold fast for the instant the flood-gates of speech. Thought is absorbed in itself.

Such is the picture we have now before us. The person around whom gathers the main interest in this narrative, has owned that weary pilgrim seated on the edge of Jacob's well, to be the promised Messiah, the Savior of the world. She remains mute under the revelation which had been made to her—she maintains expressive silence, or a silence that may have had its outlet only in tears.

Jesus, her great deliverer, who had broken the bonds of a lifetime in sunder and ushered her into glorious liberty, beholds, in this signal triumph of His grace, the *first-fruits* of a vast spiritual harvest in Samaria—the earliest trophy among the outcasts of Israel. Absorbed in the musings to which such thoughts gave birth, He, too, preserves significant silence.

The disciples have come up at the moment from their errand to the neighboring town. The last, but most momentous words of

the conversation had possibly fallen on their ears—"I who speak
unto you am He." They could not fail to observe the effect of this
disclosure. The woman's profound but suppressed emotion; the
pitchers and water-pots lying at her side, now forgotten and un-
heeded. But though by their exchanged glances, (still imbued with
the old prejudices,) they marveled that their Master talked with
this forbidden Samaritan female, there was not a word uttered—
all the three parties were thrilled and spell-bound—the *woman*, a
moment before so fluent and talkative—the *disciples*, with their
curiosity and amazement excited at the violation of national and
sectarian etiquette. But whatever might be the workings of their
inward thoughts, these are suppressed—"They were astonished to
find him talking to a woman, but none of them asked him why he
was doing it or what they had been discussing."

And the third and greatest of all, surrenders Himself more than
all, to the significant stillness of that still hour. As if unaware of
any human presence, His eye and His heart seem arrested by some
theme of distant but magnificent contemplation. "The noise of archers in the places of drawing water" is for the moment hushed;
every bow is unstrung, every rope and pitcher is at rest; the subordinate actors in the scene stand gazing on one another, while their
Lord still remains seated on the curb-stone of the well, gazing on
the fields of living green waving all around Him in that expanse
of plain, and allowing these, as we shall afterwards see, to be the
expounders and interpreters of His own heart's joy.

Very possibly the disciples, even already, were no strangers to
similar moments of absorbed contemplation on the part of their
divine Master; and though they understood not the nature of these
mysterious communings, they felt that they dared not, or would
not, intrude on their sacredness. The aged Apostle and Evangelist,
when he wrote this last Gospel, seemed to have a vivid recollec-
tion of more than one such solemn spellbinding being put upon
otherwise familiar and confidential communion. Amid the waste of
memory, he then recalled these moments of repression and significant silence at the well of Sychar; and at the close of his history, he
again records a similar inhibition put upon himself and his fellow
apostles on the occasion of the final interview on the lake-shore of
Gennesaret: "None of the disciples dare ask him, Who are you?"

Thus, we repeat, it would appear as if they were accustomed, at
special occasions, to put a restraint on their needless curiosity.
And yet, at the same time, they had learned to repose a perfect unwavering confidence in the wisdom and rectitude of their Master's

doings; they knew full well that even in these silent cogitations there were wrapped up unrevealed purposes of love and mercy. "None of the disciples dare ask him, Who are you? *knowing that it was the Lord."* These purposes might be *mysterious.* The well, like the earthly symbol at their feet, might be *deep;* yet no man said, "What do you seek?"

Although already led so far to anticipate the subject in a previous chapter, let us yet again draw the one great lesson from the words which head the present—the duty of **silence under the divine dispensations.** Often, like the disciples at Sychar, have we reason to marvel at the Lord's doings. Their marvel on this occasion arose from a poor reason, a mere sectarian and rabbinical prejudice—that their Master, who was of the tribe of Judah, should break through Jewish conventionalism by holding converse with a *female,* and that female one of the excommunicated *Samaritans.* They would, before many weeks had passed, cease their astonishment. They would have their prejudices rebuked, and their Lord's wisdom and grace vindicated.

Often have we, though in our blindness, greater reason than they had to marvel at His ways. *Providence* is often spoken of as a dark enigma. God's name, as He declared it to Manoah, is "Secret." He gives no account to any of His matters. "I the Lord dwell in the thick darkness." 'He plants his footsteps in the sea.' These footsteps are untraceable on the varying billows. They are like the wake of the vessel furrowing a momentary depression in the ocean; the dark waves close over, and not a vestige of love or wisdom is discernible—"Your way is in the sea; Your path in the deep waters, and Your footsteps are not known."

Blind unbelief, arraigning the rectitude of the divine dispensations, is prone to ask, "What do You seek in this catastrophe?" That sudden ruin of my worldly business and prospects—the heart would sincerely prompt the inquiry, 'What do You seek in this?' The pillaging of dearer household treasure—'What do You seek here?' "All you who know His name say, How is the strong staff broken, and the beautiful rod!" 'The beautiful rod,' the budding branch, the infant blossom—'What do You seek here?' These cradles emptied; these dimpled smiles turned into pale marble! Why has death not taken the seared and withered drapery from the autumn branch, but stripped the green sapling? Why not taken the browning leaves of the decaying rose, rather than the incipient bud, before the summer sun had fallen on its tints, or extracted its fragrance?

Or, stranger still, "The strong staff broken!" What do You seek here? The *beautiful rod* is missed for its beauty, but the *strong staff* is missed still more for its strength. Where is the wisdom in taking away the crutch from the arm of the *feeble*—the prop from the tottering steps of *old age?* Why thus lay the axe at the root of *manhood* in its glory? "How is the strong staff broken?" Such (say as we please) is the wailing soliloquy of many a crushed and sorrowing heart under the mystery of the Divine dealings. But the duty, the delight, the prerogative, the triumph of faith, is to be silent. "They were astonished to find Him talking to a woman, but none of them asked Him why He was doing it or what they had been discussing."

To ask no reason, no "why or wherefore;" to lie in devout submission under the inscrutable chastisement, owning, though we may be unable to discern, *the faithfulness of the great Chastener*, who often thus hides Himself and keeps silence, just in order to elicit unquestioning faith and implicit trust. What did David say, under a complication of dark individual and family trial? "I was dumb with silence; I held my peace even from good."—"I was dumb, I opened not my mouth, because You did it." What did Aaron say under a trial deeper, sadder, more overwhelming still? He said nothing—"And Aaron held his peace." What did a Greater than earthly priest or king, say in moments of mysterious suffering? "He was oppressed, and He was afflicted, yet He opened not His mouth: He is brought as a lamb to the slaughter, and as a sheep before her shearers is dumb, so He opens not His mouth."

How often is this *duty of silence* under the dealings of God, inculcated in sacred Scripture. "Rest in, the Lord, (margin, "be silent to the Lord,") and wait patiently for Him." "Truly my soul waits (or is silent) upon God." "Be silent, O all flesh, before the Lord." Or, yet again, in the sublime and striking prophecy of Habbakuk; the prophet, though appalled by the divine judgments impending on the nation and which the divine lips had themselves uttered, resolves to be silent, and to say not, "What do you seek?" He resolves to wait for further disclosures of the divine will—"I will stand upon my watch, and set myself upon the tower, and will watch to see what He will say unto me, and what I shall answer when I am reproved."

And what is God's first message to him? It is simply to continue silent—to wait. "The vision is yet for an appointed time, but at the end it shall speak and not lie: though, it tarry, wait for it; because it will surely come, it will not tarry." He compares and contrasts this silent, patient waiting, with the restless invocations of the heathen to their dumb idols—calling upon them not to be silent, but to speak—"Woe unto him that says to the wood, Awake; and to the dumb stone, Arise, it shall teach." But, he adds, "The Lord is in His holy temple; let all the earth keep silence before Him." And then this silence is only broken by the prophet's sublime prayer, in the first part of which he dwells on the mystery of God's dispensations, only that he may wind up with his grand profession of faith and trust and holy joy!

Blessed it will be for us, amid all these 'frowning providences,' if, instead of presuming in a spirit of unbelief and distrust, to ask, "What do You seek?"—we are ready to hear the voice of the Unknown and Invisible saying, "Be still, and know that I am God!" The *dutiful servant* asks no reason of his Master—he does his appointed work in silent obedience. The *loyal soldier* asks no reason of his commanding officer for what he may think the hazardous and fatal movement in the day of battle; he obeys in prompt and willing silence. The *faithful workman* asks no reason for these crude gashes in the quarry; he is content to wait until builder or sculptor fashions the unshapely block into symmetry and beauty. We are apt, with Joseph, in our blind ignorance, to say, "Not so, my Father;" but, like aged Jacob on that same occasion, *God refuses our erring dictation, our unwise counsel*, saying, "I know it, My son; I know it."

It is the grandest triumph of faith thus to confide in the divine leadings *in the dark*—when the Almighty's wings are not bright and refulgent with love and mercy and goodness, but rather projecting a mysterious shadow—then, yes, then does faith vindicate its own strength and reality, when it can utter this song in the night, "How excellent is your loving-kindness, O God; therefore the children of men put their trust under the SHADOW of your wings."

If at any time we be called to stand by some broken cistern; nothing to draw with—the rope of fond affection snapped—God's judgments 'a great deep'—be it ours to seat ourselves speechless by the brink of the shattered fountain—not marveling, not asking questions, not saying in querulous skepticism, "What do You seek?" "knowing that it is the Lord."

When Jacob crossed the brook Jabbok, (to revert, in closing, to an incident in the life of the old Patriarch, more than once already referred to,) he met, under a clear midnight sky, an angel-form—this same Redeemer. "There wrestled a man with him until the breaking of the day." There was to that solitary human wrestler a strange mysteriousness in the apparition of the magnificent visitant. He had struggled with him in the darkness; put his thigh out of joint; made him a cripple for life. But in this case, unlike the disciples at Sychar, Jacob dared not be silent. In irrepressible eagerness he asked him, and said, "Tell me, I ask you, your name?" And the other said, "Why is it that you do ask after my name?" The wrestling angel did not satisfy his curiosity by revealing his history. But he blessed him there, and sent him away, with the new name of "Israel."

Oh, how often is this true! God meeting His people in the brooding darkness of their night of trial—wrestling with them; and if they, in the deep mystery of their sorrow, are tempted to ask, "What do You seek?" He does not answer directly—He does not answer as they would like Him to answer, by desisting from the struggle. But He does better. They come out from the conflict maimed and crippled and heart-stricken it may be, but with a new name and blessing—as princes who have had power with God and prevailed.

"Come, O Traveler unknown,
Whom still I hold, but cannot see,
My company before is gone,
And I am left alone with Thee;
Wrestling, I will not let You go,
Until I Your Name, Your Nature know.

"'Tis love! 'Tis love You died for me!
I hear Your whisper in my heart!
The morning breaks, the shadows flee;
Pure universal Love You are!
To me, to all, Your affections move;
Your Nature and Your Name is love!

"The Sun of Righteousness on me
Has risen, healing in His wings;
Withered my native strength, from Thee
My soul its life and support brings
My help is all laid up above;
Your Nature and Your Name is Love!

"I know O, Savior, who You are;
Jesus, the feeble sinner's Friend!
Nor will You with the night depart,
But stay and love me to the end!
Your mercies never shall remove,

Your Nature and Your Name is Love!

"Lame as I am, I take the prey,
Hell, earth, and sin, with ease overcome;
I leap for joy, pursue my way,
And as a bounding deer fly home!
Through all eternity to prove, Your
Nature and Your Name is Love!"
—Charles Wesley, 1742.

THE HOME MISSIONARY

The woman left her water jar beside the well and went back to the village and told everyone, "Come and meet a man who told me everything I ever did! Can this be the Messiah?" So the people came streaming from the village to see him. John 4:28-30

In the former chapter, we found that the disciples had meanwhile joined their Lord at the Well, while He was still conversing with the woman of Samaria. Until now, she had enjoyed undisturbed her interview with the Divine Wayfarer; but other eyes being upon her, the conversation abruptly terminates. So it is with all our most hallowed seasons of communion with the Savior on earth. They are necessarily brief. He is to His people still, in a spiritual sense, as He was to that daughter of Israel, "as a stranger in the land, and as a wayfaring man that turns aside to tarry for a night." Blessed will that time be, when no disturbing intrusive element can interrupt the bliss of fellowship whose duration will not be a transient noontide-hour of burden and weariness, but ETERNITY!

The silence of that speechless group seems to have been first broken by the sudden departure of the woman. In the intensity of her newborn emotions she is forgetful altogether of the purpose which brought her to the well of the Patriarch; and, leaving her pitcher behind, she hastens to her native city to proclaim to her fellow-townsmen the astounding intelligence that she has found the Messiah. How altered her whole character and feelings since she left her home a brief hour before! She had left from the gates of Shechem *a miserable sinner,* she returns a rejoicing believer, with her deep spiritual thirst quenched, once and forever, at a nobler fountain.

There is something true to human nature, and truer still to the expansive, unselfish spirit of the Gospel, in seeing her thus *hastening to make others partakers of her own joy and peace.* The impulse is natural to communicate to others whatever may have imparted happiness to ourselves. A *son* who gets advancement in the world delights to take the earliest means of sending the tidings to the paternal roof. The *soldier* in the forlorn hope hastens to give to those who are waiting with breathless interest, the intelligence alike of his safety and of his feat of successful daring. The *shep-*

herd in the parable is represented, on finding the lost wanderer, as calling his friends and his neighbors together, saying, "Rejoice with me, for I have found my sheep which was lost." The *father* of the prodigal is not contented with his own happiness in giving welcome to the long absent one, but his banqueting halls are thrown open, that others may have a sympathizing participation in the gladsome return.

We may recall a moment of deeper, stranger, intenser joy still—a joy which quickened the pulses of the world's life; when *Mary Magdalene* had not only entered the deserted sepulcher, but had listened from unmistakable lips to words of wonder and gladness—with fleet step, unable to keep the ecstatic assurance to herself, she hurried to proclaim it to those most intensely interested—"She departed quickly from the sepulcher, with fear and great joy; and ran to bring His disciples word." The *two travelers to Emmaus*, when their wondering eyes were opened, hastened forthwith to the eleven with the glad news, "The Lord has risen indeed, and has appeared to Simon."

So it was in the case of the woman of Samaria. She, too, had seen her living Lord—the Messiah promised to her fathers. Her joy and wonder cannot be unshared. It was with her as with the brethren of Joseph: no sooner had the patriarch made himself known to them, saying, "I am Joseph," than they hastened to convey the startling intelligence to their aged father, "Joseph is alive!"

The *true Joseph* had made Himself known to this alien sister. She cannot keep to herself the joy of all joys. "The woman left her water jar beside the well and went back to the village and told everyone, "Come and meet a man who told me everything I ever did! Can this be the Messiah?" So the people came streaming from the village to see him."

And this is ever the true result of saving conversion, the necessary consequence of the reception of the truth into our own hearts—a longing desire to make others sharers and participators in our joy and peace in believing. If Christianity be *real* and *living,* it must be *expansive.* The work of the Spirit of God in the heart is not a fiction, not a form, but a life. To use the simile of this narrative, it is a fountain not only 'springing up,' (bubbling up,) but overflowing its cistern, and the superfluous supply going forth to gladden other waste places. Not the mass of stagnant water without outlet, but the clear, sparkling lake, discharging its rush of living streams which sing their joyous way along the contiguous valleys, and make their course known by the thread of green, beautifying and fertilizing as they flow.

Or, if we may employ another figure, let it be that whose appropriateness redeems it from commonplace—the stone thrown into the same still lake. The ripples formed are deepest in the center. Christianity is deepest in the heart in which its truths have sunk; but its influence expands in ever-widening concentric circles until the wavelets touch the shore. Religion, intensest in a man's own soul and life, should embrace family, household, kindred, neighborhood, country, until it knows no circumference but the world!

Oh, how unlike is the true spirit of the gospel to that of the world's selfishness; that selfishness which would retain *all* with tenacious, avaricious grasp, with no thought or care for the happiness or well-being of others. Christianity breaks down these walls of narrow isolation, and proclaims the true brotherhood of the race. Selfishness closes the heart, shuts out from it the rains and dews and summer sunshine; but Christianity, or rather the great Sun of light, shines—the closed petals gradually unfold in the genial beams—and they keep not their fragrance to themselves, but waft it all around. Every such flower, the smallest that blushes unseen to the world—becomes a little censer swinging its incense-perfume in the silent air, or sending it far and wide by the passing breeze.

The woman of Samaria became, as every Christian who has tasted and seen that the Lord is gracious ought to become, a *home evangelist and missionary*. Origen calls her "the apostle of the Samaritans." The entire words in the song of an elder sister in Israel, which we have more than once partially quoted, are beautifully true in her case with reference to the inhabitants of her city: "Those who are delivered from the noise of archers in the places of drawing water, there shall they rehearse the righteous acts of the Lord, even the righteous acts towards the inhabitants of his villages in Israel: then shall the people of the Lord go down to the gates."

And her case and character are, in this respect, only in beautiful keeping and harmony with manifold examples in sacred Scripture—"going down to the gates," and proclaiming to others, "This gate of the Lord into which the righteous shall enter." *Job* was such a missionary. Not content himself with knowing and rejoicing in the revelation of a 'living Redeemer,' that evangelist of the Arabian desert, in words appropriate to his barren home, expresses his ardent desire that others might participate in the glorious discovery, "Oh that my words were now written! oh that they were printed in a book! that they were engraved with an iron pen and lead in the rock forever!"

David was such a missionary. The tokens of God's forgiving grace and mercy vouchsafed to himself, acted as a stimulus and incentive to convey these to others, "Then will I teach transgressors Your ways, and sinners shall be converted unto You"—"Come, all you who fear God, I will declare what He has done for my soul."

Andrew was such a missionary. For, having himself beheld and welcomed the Lamb of God, we read, "The first thing Andrew did was to find his brother Simon and tell him, "We have found the Messiah" (that is, the Christ). And he brought him to Jesus."

Philip was such a missionary. Himself the recipient of the glad news, he "finds Nathaniel, and said unto him, We have found Him of whom Moses in the law, and the prophets wrote, Jesus of Nazareth" at the same time extracting from the simple-hearted Jew, the noble avowal, "Rabbi, You are the Son of God; You are the King of Israel."

The converted *maniac of Gadara* became such a missionary. He was not permitted to continue his posture, "sitting at the feet of Jesus, clothed and in his right mind," a passive subject of the wondrous transformation—"Jesus sent him away, saying, Return to your own house and show how great things God has done to you. And he went his way, and published throughout the whole city how great things Jesus had done unto him."

And so it was also with the greatest of all converted men. No sooner was *Paul* struck to the ground by the heavenly light, and heard the voice of that Jesus whom so long he had persecuted, than he "immediately preached Christ in the synagogues of Damascus, that He is the Son of God." "You," says Christ, *to all* and *of all* His people—"you are the light of the world." As little can the sun retain his heat to himself, or the moon her borrowed luster, as the believer cease to be a radiating center of holy influence. "If these should hold their peace, the stones would immediately cry out." And if this influence, in the case of not a few, fail of being of an active nature, let all remember that there is one of another kind equally acceptable to God, and equally potent for good. The Christian, confined for weary years to a sickbed, is rendered physically incapable of the outer activities of the spiritual life; but there is *a speechless eloquence and power in a holy, Christlike character.* Such may prove silent evangelists, commending the gospel to others by their meek, patient, enduring, unmurmuring resignation—like the alabaster box of old, broken unnoticed and unobserved;

but the whole house, (the little sphere of their influence), is filled with the odor of the ointment!

To return to the narrative. The mission of this female evangelist was signally **successful**. For it is added, "So the people came streaming from the village to see Him." Now there is something in this statement which is remarkable, and well worthy of our attention. She has made a startling assertion in the midst of those who were only too cognizant of her character. Yet they credit her testimony; they obey, apparently with alacrity, her summons, and crowd with her to see the Judean Pilgrim. With some of these, doubtless, there may have been no higher motive or inducement than curiosity; but from the sequel, we seem warranted to infer that this was not the predominant reason. They had given a ready and hearty credence to the wondrous story of this strangest of attesting witnesses, and at her bidding, and under her guidance, they hasten without hesitation to the old traditional Well.

What could it have been which rendered her testimony so strong, so self-evidencing and self-authenticating? We may note one or two particulars which must have specially tended to conquer their prejudices, and prepare them for a recognition of these same Messiah-claims.

(1.) Her **honesty** and outspoken candor must have gained her a favorable hearing: "Come," she said, "see a man that told me all things that ever I did." It was the last thing we could have expected her to utter—the last message they would have expected her to deliver—to ask them to come to see one whose penetrating glance had read and revealed her blackened history. She would in ordinary circumstances have shrunk from such *a revelation of herself.* Indeed, when we see her leaving the well and disappearing among the old olive trees on the road to the city, the natural suggestion which occurs to us is, that she is glad to rush away from the withering glance and exposure of that Heart-searcher, saying, in the spirit of the oldest world-transgressor, "I heard your voice, and I was afraid, because I was naked; and I hid myself."

We expect that if she makes any reference at all to the mysterious stranger, it would be by doing what she could to keep others from going to listen, possibly to fresh disclosures of her character and vicious life; that if she said anything to her fellow-citizens about that Jewish traveler, it would rather be to depreciate His authority and turn into ridicule His words and similitudes. But this, on the contrary, is the very point on which she emphatically dwells. This is to her the credential of His Messiahship, that He has told her all her nefarious past history—that He is fully acquainted with her life of sin.

Could this honest avowal fail to carry its own moral weight to the minds of these simple, straightforward villagers or townsmen of Sychar—that despite of these disclosures, instead of evading Him—belittling Him—mocking Him—throwing discredit on His claims, or keeping the strange interview of that morning a profound secret locked up in her heart of hearts, she invites them to come and see Him, and hear for themselves His omniscient and searching words?

(2.) Another thing which must have won for her the attention of her fellow-citizens, was her **earnestness**. "Come!" she said, with inviting urgency. Her strange assertions might at first be met by obstinacy and scorn. She might probably at first be regarded as a raving enthusiast and fanatic—the victim of some sudden bewildering phantasm, possessed with one of the demons of their false spirit worship; or perhaps as subserving some hypocritical ends—a deceiver, and being deceived. But probably her tears and heartfelt genuine penitence, coupled with the transparent veracity of her statement, satisfied them that there was in her case no pretense, no delusion.

There was about her tale and her manner an indubitable reality, which conquered and annihilated the strength even of Samaritan prejudices. She may have appeared at first, like Lot to his sons-in-law, "as one that mocks." But in abrupt, importunate earnestness, the smitten penitent implores them to go and see—to go and judge for themselves. These pleadings are irresistible. They went out of the city, she herself probably accompanying them, "and came unto Him." *What is to compare with earnestness?* There is a true ring about it which cannot be simulated or counterfeited. *What Christian ministry, what Christian life, so powerful as an earnest one?* It is not the *charm of intellect*, not the *subtlety of reasoning*, not the *magic of eloquence*, that will commend the gospel to others. It is the living words welling up from the believing soul, the lips uttering and proclaiming what has been experimentally felt and tested. "I believed, therefore have I spoken."

Unsanctified intellect has often preached an unknown Savior. Strange as it may seem, unsanctified intellect has even at times not delivered its message in vain, just as the trumpet which stirs the hearts of the brave in battle may be sounded by coward or unworthy lips. But the ministry and the mission most signally owned and blessed by the great Master, is not the wisdom of human words, or the grandeur of flowery orations, but where there is the irresistible cogency of *living fervor*. Men of the world are quick-sighted enough to penetrate the flimsy veil of unreality and pretension, to discover those who are the mere imposters in the great army of the brave and the true.

On the other hand, where there is unction and reality, other deficiencies will be overlooked and palliated. Even intellectual superiority willingly stoops to hear *the heartfelt tale*, though it may be delivered with unlettered and stammering tongue. Hence, in the Gospels, the two most honored of preachers, with the exception of the Baptist, just because their tongues were touched with burning earnestness, were that *converted demoniac of Gadara,* and *this converted woman of Samaria.* Oh for an earnest Church and an earnest ministry! the baptism "with the Holy Spirit and with fire!"

(3.) We may add one other impression which must have been made upon the people of Shechem—the effect which that mysterious interview at the Well had upon the woman herself. It had made her **happy**. He had told her all things that ever she did. That, we might have thought, and so would they, should have had the effect of making her wretched. We know the awful feeling which another's cognizance of some crimson sin inspires. It makes the transgressor miserable. Hush-money is the well-known human quietus of a troubled conscience—the ready bribe to muffle the anguish of discovered wrong-doing—the key which locks up the terrible secret. But this woman's guilty secrets were out and disclosed—One Infinite yet human heart at least knew them all. He knew the worst of her. He was within a mile of where she now was—yet she was happy!

Among these half heathen Shechemites were there no spiritual burdens as heavy to be borne as her own? Do we think, amid these rough hewers of wood and drawers of water, there were none of the world's aching hearts to be found? Would they not willingly too pass through the same ordeal as she, if only the oppressive load could be removed? Would they not willingly brave the scrutiny of this omniscient One, and allow Him to unlock their deepest secrets, if only the storm, as in her case, could be changed into a calm by His omnipotent, "Peace, be still?"

Such, then, being the credentials of this female messenger, let us glance at the subject of her MESSAGE. This, too, is remarkable and worthy of note; for in it she tells her fellow-citizens the very fact which we might have expected she would have withheld, and she omits what we would have expected her rather to proclaim. We expect, as she enters Sychar, and gathers the wondering crowd around her, to hear her speak of what we deem alike the most beautiful and the most memorable part of her story—that, too, which would be most impressive to the Oriental mind—about the Well, the thirst, the living water, the gift of God, everlasting life. Or if not this, the mystic sayings about Gerizim and Zion, the world-wide worship, the revelation of the Great Father.

Not a word is said of any of these; no, not even does she speak of the stranger's own closing avowal of his Messiahship. The one declaration—that which has stirred her heart to its depths (she seems to have room for no other) is this, "He told me all things that ever I did." As in the case of Felix, when a greater than Paul now spoke of 'temperance, righteousness, and the judgment to come,' *conscience spoke*, and her immortal spirit trembled! And as in speaking of the Christian ministry we have adverted to one element at least of persuasive power in the character of the messenger, so have we here the most effective and influential characteristic of his message. It is not figurative expositions, not controversial disputes, not subtle metaphysical distinctions about the nature and character of God, but the direct commending of the truth to the conscience; awakening a deep sense of sin—rousing the soul to a consciousness of the virulence of its disease, and thus preparing it for a revelation of the one glorious remedy.

It was asserted by divine lips to be the first part of the Holy Spirit's work in conversion, "He will convince the world of sin." The evidences of the *schools* are not without their peculiar value—but the stateliest array of these will never of themselves bring home conviction to one heart. They are not what prove most effectual in gathering in wanderers to the fold—they are not the pitchers which fetch up from the well of life its reviving draughts.

That rather which wins and arrests and conquers, is the knowledge which the Bible has of *myself*, in telling me "all things that ever I did"—the adaptation of the Great Physician to the wounds and heart-sores of aching humanity—the adaptation of the living water to the thirsty soul. This is the history of every drawer of that water—"God who commanded the light to shine out of darkness, has shone in our hearts, to give the light of the knowledge of the glory of God in the face of Jesus Christ."

The Great Teacher, 'the teller of all things,' the true "Word of God," is a "discerner of the thoughts and the intents of the heart." The gracious words to ancient Israel collectively, seem to have a special beauty and significance in their application to this individual case of the Samaritan woman—a comment on the later saying, "Where sin abounded grace did much more abound."—"She decked herself with her earrings and her jewels, and she went after her lovers, and forgot me, says the Lord. Therefore, behold, I will allure her and bring her into the *wilderness*, and will speak comfortably unto her." (lit. speak to her heart.)

A gospel faith is the response of the human spirit within, to the Revelation without. The unlettered Christian can confront bold skepticism, and fight it with this "proved sword," this unanswerable argument, "Come, see a man who told me all things that ever I did!" "One thing I know, that whereas I was blind, now I see."

Let us close with one practical remark, **the power of feeble influences.** If it has been a matter of interest to us to watch the dealing of Christ with an individual sinner at the well of Jacob, more interesting still is the sequel we have been now considering—the crowd, appearing among the trees, of anxious seeking souls, coming to test for themselves the truth of the wondrous tidings, and to prefer the prayer—"Lord, give us this water that we thirst not!" But it is of further interest and significance to note, that this flocking of the people of Shechem to listen to the Divine Stranger was the result of the pleadings and urgency of *one feeble woman.* She herself had become, to use the beautiful figure of the Psalmist, as a dove whose wings are covered with silver, and her feathers with yellow gold. In the freshness of her heavenly plumage, this *dove of Samaria* flies immediately with the olive branch in her mouth to her own Shechem valley, not to seek with folded pinion some quiet perch on Gerizim, but rather to hasten her flight back again to the *true Noah*, the Giver of "Rest," bringing along with her a flock with weary wing and wailing cry. "Who are these that fly as a cloud, and as the doves to their windows?"

Never let us undervalue feeble instrumentality! It was the blast of rams' horns, accompanied with the shout of the army of Israel, which brought to the ground the walls of Jericho. It was the crash of three hundred pitchers and the gleam of torches by the well of Jezreel, accompanied by the battle-cry, "The sword of the Lord and of Gideon," which routed the mighty host of the Midianites. It was a few pebbles from the running brook, and a sling in the hands of a shepherd boy, which laid low the giant of Philistia.

Let none make the *feebleness of their efforts* in the Church of Christ the reason for neglecting or abandoning them. Let none make the *smallness of their talent* a reason for burying it in the earth; but rather put it out to interest, that when their Lord comes

He may receive His own with interest. *It is by small and often insignificant means He still effects the mightiest of His purposes* in His Church on earth. He would make this still the motive to all exertion—the secret of all success—the watchword to every Faint-heart and Ready-to-halt in the day of battle—"Not by might nor by power, but by my Spirit, says the Lord of hosts."

THE HEAVENLY FOOD AND THE FIELD OF HARVEST

Meanwhile his disciples urged him, "Rabbi, eat something." But He said to them, "I have food to eat that you know nothing about." Then His disciples said to each other, "Could someone have brought Him food?" "My food," said Jesus, "is to do the will of Him who sent me and to finish His work. Do you not say, 'Four months more and then the harvest'? I tell you, open your eyes and look at the fields! They are ripe for harvest. Even now the reaper draws his wages, even now he harvests the crop for eternal life, so that the sower and the reaper may be glad together. Thus the saying 'One sows and another reaps' is true. I sent you to reap what you have not worked for. Others have done the hard work, and you have reaped the benefits of their labor." John 4:31-38

The departure of the woman of Samaria to communicate her tidings of wonder and joy to her fellow-citizens in Shechem introduces us to a second scene in the shifting drama of the narrative. Up to this point the whole interest is concentrated in the conversation between her and the Savior. Now it is between Jesus and His returned disciples. They are once more alone. The verses which head this chapter are so full of material for thought, that little more can be done than to give a running commentary upon them, leaving the reader to fill in with details the outline of the suggestive picture.

The adorable Redeemer, as we have previously seen, was seated on the brink of the Well, absorbed in mysterious contemplation. No one ventured to intrude on His sacred musings. "Just then his disciples arrived. They were astonished to find Him talking to a woman, but none of them asked Him why He was doing it or what they had been discussing." The disciples now resolve to break silence. They observe His wan and weary countenance. They know that He cannot fail to be hungry, with His fast unbroken since the early morning meal, and with the long and toilsome travel through the hot plain. With earnest imploring accents they asked Him to partake of their provided refreshment, "In the meanwhile His disciples urging Jesus to eat." Their request was apparently disregarded. With His eye and soul still riveted in these mystic communings, He replies in the enigmatical words, "I have food to eat that you know not of."

The disciples looked at each other in perplexity. Though they may have heard the last words of the conversation with the woman, they were in entire ignorance as yet of its results; they said one to another, "Has any man brought Him anything to eat?" 'Has His hunger been satisfied in our absence?—has some passing wayfarer shared his food with Him?—or has this Samaritan drawer of water so far overcome her sectarian scruples as to minister to His needs? Or has He departed in the present case from His usual measures, and called in the exercise of supernatural means? Has He summoned, as His great prophet of Cherith, the ravens from Ebal or the silver plumaged doves of Gerizim to be His suppliers?—or have angels, as in the Mount of Temptation, been sent to Him to strengthen Him?'

Poor earthly dreamers! they had utterly failed to grasp the meaning and grandeur of His saying; the material thoughts which for the moment were occupying them, prevented them fathoming these profound musings. They had nothing to draw with, and the well was deep. His reference was to food of a far different kind—"Man does not live by bread alone." Who can wonder, as Augustine well observes, at the 'inability of the ignorant, uninstructed Samaritan woman, in the previous interaction, to comprehend the spiritual symbol of the living water, when the Savior's own disciples manifest a similar inability to comprehend the meaning of the living bread! But He bears with their lack of spiritual discernment; He upbraids them not; but rather, we may imagine, His face suffused with joy, He continues in a tone of sublime mystery, "My food is to do the will of Him who sent me, and to finish His work."

It was another noble utterance. The whole grandeur of the scheme of Redemption seemed, as in a vision or trance of glory, to pass at that moment before His eyes—the work that was to be finished on the cross by giving Himself a ransom for the world—bringing up the living water by the golden cord of His everlasting love, in order that perishing millions might be saved forever. It was the partaking of these streams of salvation by one of these millions, (the unlikeliest unit among them all,) which had given birth to these divine meditations. We have already noted the suggestive silence which closed the preceding interview: such silence, we found, as is often the result, or attendant of strong emotional feeling. The same mental agitation his been known, not infrequently, to put a temporary arrest on the demands of bodily hunger.

There are great crisis-hours—times whether of yearning affection or of patriot valor—when the whole nature being in a paroxysm of suspense, the pangs of physical hunger are overborne and suppressed. The brave *leader* in the beleaguered fort or garrison, where the lives of hundreds are staked on a few hours or days of heroic resistance, is sustained by doing his duty—the cravings of the lower nature are subordinated, for the time being, to the demands of the higher. Or the *mother*, when her child is being rescued from the surging waves, can stand hunger-stricken for hours together on the bleak shore; the food which sympathizing hands have brought lies untouched at her side, as she watches with eager gaze the return of suspended animation—the revivifying of her withered flower—the call of hunger is forgotten until she is relieved from her agonizing vigil by the glad word, "Your child lives."

He who was "bone of our bone," partaker of our nature in all its finer and grander emotions, surrenders Himself here to the same absorbing power. He rises, in these magnificent musings of obedience and love, above the sensation of bodily hunger. The meal procured in the Samaritan town is laid at His side, but He heeds it not; another banquet of better *spiritual* food rivets His thoughts; another Gerizim—another Mount of imperishable blessing rises before Him—"And on this mountain the Lord Almighty will spread a wonderful feast for everyone around the world. It will be a delicious feast of good food, with clear, well-aged wine and choice beef. In that day he will remove the cloud of gloom, the shadow of death that hangs over the earth. He will swallow up death forever! The Sovereign Lord will wipe away all tears."

And here we have to note a new turn in the conversation. A new object seems at this moment to arrest observation and to offer fresh food and theme for holy joy. As He gazes along the wide green plain in the direction of Shechem, a crowd appears in the distance. He does not require to be informed of whom that crowd is composed; for His omniscient eye has followed the woman in her mission to her fellow-townsmen, and He now recognizes her returning at their head, towards the spot which had so hallowed a place in her own dearest memories. He resumes His divine discourse, and secures afresh the attention of His wondering disciples by quoting a Galilean proverb to these men of Galilee.

It is worthy of note, how largely the Divine Redeemer, in His sayings and discourses, loved to use the *book of nature* as the interpreter of the volume of grace. We know how His parables teem with pages from that volume. He loved to make the outer natural world a consecrated medium for the illumination and illustration of spiritual verities. He had done so already in the previous part of this conversation at the well. He had taken the *water* to symbolize what alone could quench the thirst of the deathless spirit. He had taken the *bread*, which the disciples had laid on its stone margin, and made it speak of higher realities—the sustaining power derived from the consciousness of doing God's will and finishing His work. And now, as once more He looks around Him on the magnificent plain flushed with the green of early spring—an unbroken expanse of verdure—He takes this beautiful page in the same illuminated book of nature, as the exponent of the great thoughts that were burdening His soul—"Do you not say [in other words, are not you accustomed to this proverbial saying], 'Four months more and then the harvest'? I tell you, open your eyes and look at the fields! They are ripe for harvest."

He passed from the green sprouting corn all around, to the glorious fullness of a *spiritual ingathering*, whose first ripe sheaf in the person of the Samaritan woman had that day been reaped. As if He had said, 'In this present case of better spiritual reaping, it is not as in the natural world where development is gradual, where the grain is ripened and matured by slow invisible processes—first the blade, then the ear, then the full corn in the ear. Here is a more glorious harvest ready—a harvest of souls—a people born in a day—in the fields of unpromising Samaria the reaper-angels may already put in their sickles, for the harvest is ripe. The glory of Lebanon has been given to it, the excellency of Carmel and Sharon; it has seen the glory of the Lord and the excellency of our God.'

But it would be a restricted and imperfect view of these divine reflections—these ecstatic thoughts and emotions, did we regard them as evoked merely by the appearance of that handful of approaching Shechemites. He regards such only as the representatives of a vaster throng, the first-fruits of a redeemed multitude which no man can number, who are to be gathered at the great harvest of the world. He sees now a handful of corn on the top of these mountains of Ephraim, but the fruit thereof is one day to shake like Lebanon, and they of the city to flourish like grass of the earth. They are the Eshcol-pledges of a far more glorious vintage. Perhaps, in the language here employed, He may be instituting a comparison between the woman with her fellow-Samaritans, and the green fields around yet untouched with the latter rains, and on which the glow of harvest was yet far off, though it would in due time surely come. That company of human souls formed the early seed sown; but in them, as through a telescopic glass, He beheld in prophetic vista the bounteous fields of the wide world waving in their summer and autumn glory.

This was the true interpretation of His enigmatical words—this was the food which those at His side knew not of. Under the shadow of the great mountain of blessing before one of the holy places of nature's gigantic temple, He, the great High Priest, waves the sheaf of first-fruits. It is the pledge and harbinger of a glorious reaping-time at the final harvest, when He, the Man of sorrows, now going forth weeping bearing precious seed, would doubtless come again with rejoicing, bringing His sheaves with Him.

The spectacle before His eyes inspires Him with a new longing and incentive to finish His work. He sees of the fruit of the travail of His soul, and is satisfied. A later saying seems already to stir the depths of His divine emotional nature: "But I have a baptism to undergo, and how distressed I am until it is completed!" But (to complete this rapid paraphrase of the verses yet remaining) though His own soul is thus full of joy—though He is Himself the mighty Sower—the Author and Finisher of the faith, in that hour of glowing anticipation He embraced also His own disciples, and through them all His faithful harvest-men and reapers, who, to the end of time, were to be subordinately associated with Him in bringing many sons unto glory. Great also, He declares, will be their joy and reward, "And he that reaps receives wages, and gathers fruit unto life eternal."

Oh, noble thought and recompense for all Christ's true servants, struggling, toiling, baffled, and discouraged! The Master says, "He gathers fruit unto life eternal." The toiler of earth has only an earthly recompense. That recompense, moreover, is uncertain, capricious, precarious. The drought may leave the harvest sickles hanging rusting on the walls, or a sudden wave of calamity may come and sweep the harvest of a lifetime away. But the spiritual laborer sows and reaps for eternity! Reaping, too, beyond the reach of casualty or disaster. No shortcoming in the garners of immortality; no blight to mock his hopes; no failure to defraud him of his harvest joy. And, better than all, it is added, "Both he that sows, and he that reaps, shall rejoice together"—the Master and the servant, the Lord and disciple.

In the great reaping day of Judgment, when every faithful harvestman will be called to receive his reward, and when *fidelity, not success*, will form the ground of approval, this will be the no-blest—the peerless element in the recompense, "Enter into the joy of your Lord." "They rejoice before You according to the joy in harvest, and as men rejoice when they divide the spoil."

The writer of these pages vividly recalls the last glimpse he took of the Well of Jacob, with Mount Gerizim rising behind in its sky of cloudless azure. The lines of a simple but well-known hymn, prized more on account of child memories, than for their own, intrinsic excellence, occurred at the time. Their otherwise enigmatical emblems seemed, amid these surroundings at least, to be invested with new meaning and significance. They may appropriately end these chapters, as we, too, take our last mental glimpse of the same hallowed spot, suggesting in symbol a better Fountain, and the Gerizim of truer spiritual blessings.

They are lines which might befittingly have been put into the lips of the woman of Samaria herself—the once lost, but now reclaimed 'wanderer from the fold'—as we may picture her at times stealing out alone to the place of her spiritual birth, standing by the well with all its consecrated remembrances, and with the knowledge that Gerizim and Zion were henceforth to be displaced and superseded by a nobler Mountain—that of 'God's unchanging love!'

Come, Thou Fount of every blessing,
Tune my heart to sing Thy grace;
Streams of mercy, never ceasing,
Call for songs of loudest praise.

Teach me some melodious sonnet,
Sung by flaming tongues above.
Praise the mount! I'm fixed upon it,
Mount of Thy redeeming love.

Here I raise my Ebenezer;
Here by Thy great help I've come;
And I hope, by Thy good pleasure,
Safely to arrive at home.

Jesus sought me when a stranger,
Wandering from the fold of God;
He, to rescue me from danger,
Interposed His precious blood.

O to grace how great a debtor
Daily I'm constrained to be!

Let Thy goodness, like a fetter,
Bind my wandering heart to Thee.

Prone to wander, Lord, I feel it,
Prone to leave the God I love;
Here's my heart, O take and seal it,
Seal it for Thy courts above.

O that day when freed from sinning,
I shall see Thy lovely face;
Clothed then in blood washed linen
How I'll sing Thy sovereign grace.

Come, my Lord, no longer tarry,
Take my ransomed soul away;
Send thine angels now to carry
Me to realms of endless day.

CPSIA information can be obtained
at www.ICGtesting.com
Printed in the USA
BVOW08s0717220417
481752BV00004B/5/P